Political Justice in Budapest after World War II

Political Justice in Budapest after World War II

Ildikó Barna and Andrea Pető

Central European University Press
Budapest – New York

© 2015 Ildikó Barna, Andrea Pető

Published in 2015 by
Central European University Press
An imprint of the
Central European University Limited Liability Company
Nádor utca 11, H-1051 Budapest, Hungary
Tel: +36-1-327-3138 or 327-3000
Fax: +36-1-327-3183
E-mail: ceupress@ceu.hu
Website: www.ceupress.com
224 West 57th Street, New York, NY 10019, USA
Tel: +1-212-547-6932
Fax: +1-646-557-2416
E-mail: meszarosa@ceu.hu

All rights reserved. No part of this publication may be reproduced, stored in a retrieval system, or transmitted, in any form or by any means, without the permission of the Publisher.

ISBN 978-963-386-052-6 cloth

ISBN 978-615-5225-98-7 paperback

Library of Congress Cataloging-in-Publication Data

Barna, Ildikó, author.
[Politikai igazságszolgáltatás a II. világháború utáni Budapesten. English]
Political justice in Budapest after World War II / Ildikó Barna and Andrea Pető.
pages cm
Includes bibliographical references and index.
ISBN 978-9633860526 (hardbound)
1. Hungary. Népbíróság. 2. Justice, Administration of--Hungary--History. 3. Trials (Political crimes and offenses)--Hungary--History. 4. Jews--Legal status, laws, etc.--Hungary. I. Peto, Andrea, author. II. Title.
KKF1593.C65B3713 2014
345.439'0231094391209044--dc23
2014016285

Contents

List of Figures	vii
Foreword	1
Political Justice in Europe: The State of Research	7
Legal Background to the People's Tribunals and Their Operation in Hungary	13
The System of People's Tribunals and the Actors in the Process	17
The Crimes and the Range of Punishments	21
Controversies Surrounding the Law on People's Tribunals	23
Research Methodology	27
Method of Approach	27
Preparation Phase	29
Pilot research	29
Expert roundtable	30
Training of the Encoders	32
The Final Questionnaire	32
Research Phase	33
Sampling procedure	34
From filling in the questionnaires to the data files	34
Preparing the data files for analysis	37
Several Notes on the Methodology and the Findings	41
Analysis of the People's Tribunal Cases	45
Types of Cases	45
Distribution of the types of cases over time	47
Characteristics of the Case Files	49
Analysis of the Various Actors in the People's Tribunals	50
Defendants	50
Gender Ratios	51
Age distribution	52
Place of birth	53
Level of education	55

Social status	56
Membership in the Arrow Cross	58
Witnesses	60
Gender ratios	61
Age distribution	62
Place of birth	63
Social status	64
Summary of the Demographics of Defendants and Witnesses in the Various Types of Cases	65
Lawyers	69
Characteristics of the People's Tribunal Cases	71
The length of trials and the number of hearings	71
The role of witnesses at the people's tribunals	72
Judgments	77
Effect of the composition of witnesses on judgments	82

A Gendered Analysis of Political Justice in Hungary in the Aftermath of World War II — 85

Women in Political Justice: Stereotypes and Reality about Women Perpetrators	86
Witnesses	90
Court Judgments	92
Women People's Judges	93
Summary: Gender in Political Justice	96

Jewish Identity and the People's Tribunals — 97

Characteristics of the People's Tribunal Cases	98
Defendants and Their Characteristics	101
Witnesses and Their Characteristics	102
Court Judgments	104
Jewish Identity and the Practice of Political Justice	104

Summary	111
Bibliography	115
Index	121

List of Figures

Figure 3.1	Sample of data file at the level of the case files	39
Figure 3.2	Sample of data file at the level of defendants	40
Figure 4.1	Types of trials	47
Figure 4.2	Types of trials over time	48
Figure 4.3	Content of the case files	49
Figure 4.4	Gender ratios of defendants by trial types and in the whole sample, and gender ratio of the general population	51
Figure 4.5	Age distribution of defendants by trial types and in the whole sample, and age distribution of the general population	53
Figure 4.6	Birthplace distribution of defendants by trial types and in the whole sample, and birthplace distribution of the general population	54
Figure 4.7	Educational level of defendants by trial types and in the whole sample, and educational level of the general population	56
Figure 4.8	Social status of defendants by trial types and in the whole sample, and social status of the general population	58
Figure 4.9	Defendants by membership of Arrow Cross in the whole sample and by trial types	60
Figure 4.10	Number of witnesses in the whole sample and by trial types	61
Figure 4.11	Gender ratios of witnesses by trial types and in the whole sample, and gender ratio of the general population	62
Figure 4.12	Age distribution of witnesses by trial types and in the whole sample, and age distribution of the general population	63
Figure 4.13	Birthplace distribution of witnesses by trial types and in the whole sample, and birthplace distribution of the general population	64
Figure 4.14	Social status of witnesses by trial types and in the whole sample, and social status of the general population	65
Figure 4.15	Comparison of gender ratios of defendants and witnesses by trial types and witnesses	66
Figure 4.16	Comparison of age distributions of defendants and witnesses by trial types	67
Figure 4.17	Comparison of birthplaces of defendants and witnesses by trial types	68
Figure 4.18	Comparison of social status of defendants and witnesses by trial types	69
Figure 4.19	Appointed public defenders and paid lawyers by trial types	70
Figure 4.20	Number of hearings in the whole sample and by trial types	72
Figure 4.21	Ratios of supporting and incriminating witnesses in the whole sample and by trial types	73
Figure 4.22	Ratios of valuable and not valuable statements in the whole sample and by trial types	74
Figure 4.23	Two-dimensional typology of statements in the whole sample and by trial types	76
Figure 4.24	Acquittals and convictions in the whole sample and by trial types	78
Figure 5.1	Age distribution of defendants by gender and by the time of crime; gender and age distribution of the general population	88
Figure 5.2	Educational level of defendants in the whole sample and by gender; age and educational level of the general population aged 20 or over	90
Figure 5.3	Age distribution of witnesses in the whole sample and by gender; gender and age distribution of the general population	91
Figure 5.4	Ratios of female people's judges by trial types and in the whole sample	94

Foreword

For political justice in post-World War II Hungary, there is both a history and a memory. The two aspects have less and less in common. This conflict explains why we embarked upon this basic research. Though the literature on the people's tribunals (a selection of which is given in the bibliography) is growing, its effect on public discourse and in public life has been negligible. The primary reason for this lies in the distinction drawn between history and public history. While public history addresses a broader audience in order to achieve some specific aim, "history" seeks to meet the standards of an audience which it calls professional. The history of the people's tribunals is a field dominated by professional historians, and the knowledge gained has not influenced in a meaningful way the public discourse about the tribunals. A second reason is the theoretical framework within which research is undertaken and interpreted. The people's tribunals were a means for establishing justice after World War II; both their appraisal and the interpretation of their role tend to be politicized. Political fracture lines determine evaluations of the justice system and preclude the proper consideration of positions that do not fit the political frame. The third reason is that around 1 in 10 Hungarians have personal knowledge of cases tried by the people's tribunals: either they themselves were witnesses or defendants in such cases, or the transitional justice process affected someone in the family who then told other family members of his or her experiences. In this way, stories have been passed down from one generation to the next, and these stories have little in common with the history textbook accounts of the people's tribunals. Some of these personal stories are the accounts of individuals who were indicted and tried by the tribunals for their actions during World War II. Consequently, they developed in opposition to the dominant anti-fascist discourse, while the authenticity of personal experience lent them their weight. Thus we see a competition, or rivalry, between two public histories, which ends in the defeat of the anti-fascist discourse, whereafter the levels of argumentation coalesce and it becomes less and less clear that crimes really were committed during World War II for which people needed to be held to account.

According to Jon Elster, various forms of punishment and retribution are employed at times of transition: exclusion (marginalization), targeted killing, the screening of professional organizations, the imposition of sanctions against state officials who collaborated with the previous regime, the public humiliation of guilty parties, and public trials (Elster 2006, 33). In Hungary, lynching and public vilification and humiliation were avoided. The country did not have a powerful partisan movement, which in France, Italy, and Bulgaria had arbitrarily executed or variously humiliated collaborators (e.g., by publicly shaving women's heads) in the immediate aftermath of liberation. In Hungary, the screening of professional organizations, investigations into the pasts of state officials, and trials were the means of transition. Each of these forms of action and punishment mediated such emotions as hatred, contempt, and shame. And this mediation took place at the level of the individual participants in the process. For this reason, transitional justice cannot be examined without analysis at the micro level. But such micro-level analysis can be misleading; it not only fails to give us a full picture but also influences what is visible to us.

How does the justice system influence what is recorded in the public memory? According to Markovits, there are two ways of investigating this issue (Markovits 2001). The first is the institutionalist approach: it is claimed that the operation of the system was not independent of political power, and so the task is to examine how the institutions of the justice system applied the laws in force. The problem with this approach is that any conclusions drawn are based primarily on documents created by the institutions themselves. Yet, any legal system follows a given ideology, and the extent of this will change over time. This approach does not take into consideration the individuals who applied the law within the given framework or the individuals who were drawn into the system and who attempted, using the means at their disposal, to obtain whatever was for them the most favorable outcome (judgment or sentence). Alf Lüdtke called this the *Eigen-Sinn* (see Markovits 2001, 547), which could be translated as "will" or "stubbornness." In the English-speaking world, this is called *agency*, whereby individuals can leave their mark on the actions of the state. In the literature the institutional historical approach is usually linked with an analysis of individual cases, which within this investigative framework immediately become "atypical."

The other investigative approach is to listen to and evaluate "victims' stories." The number of such stories increased rapidly after 1989, and they have become the dominant public historical discourse. As a result, the dominant and uncritical anti-fascist discourse has gradually been replaced by a stricter critique of the people's tribunals and the process they represented. The victims' stories stir emotions by presenting individual sufferings. Indeed, emotions assume a key role, even though they offer us few insights into the great historical processes and tend to direct our attention to the need to compensate victims for what has happened to them. The stories emerging in recent years about the people's tribunals tell inevitably of the sufferings of the pre-World War II elite, whose accounts, given the complex workings of human memory, are not the real story but rather a version of it containing those things that may be told from their perspective. These stories have a further grave consequence: the only accounts we hear are those of the elite, while the stories of the many ordinary victims are silenced. Indeed, their stories are removed from public memory, and we are left with a mosaic-like impression of events.

In this book we endeavor—in contrast with earlier approaches—to examine the history of the people's tribunals by means of a new methodology that we ourselves have elaborated. Seeking to rise above ideological considerations and the methodological problems of earlier investigative frameworks, we hope to bring about a new level of awareness. We look at the legal history of the people's tribunals from 1945 to 1949, focusing our research on this era. We do not concern ourselves with the role of people's tribunals in the post-1956 period, as this would distract us from our primary task: to gain a clear understanding of the functioning of political justice in the immediate aftermath of World War II. Thus in our investigation we consider the period 1945–1949 to have constituted a separate era. Assisted by a strict and consistent quantitative methodology, we seek to determine which people were drawn into the transitional justice process and how the people's tribunals functioned, with particular regard to gendered aspects. A further aim is to reveal the effects of the people's tribunals on post-Holocaust Jewish identity.

In the literature, evaluations of the people's tribunals tend to be dichotomic: justice versus revenge (or retaliation). In this volume, we intend to step out of this dichotomy and present the workings of a complex process we call the people's tribunals process. With our newfound knowledge of the workings of the tribunals, we hope to be able—based on "objective" data—to draw novel conclusions concerning the process as a whole. In our understanding, the operation of the people's tribunals is a legal process characterized by both continuity and discontinuity. On the basis of the documents created during the process, however, it is possible to make valid statements concerning its functioning.

In the literature, there is a growing tendency to view the people's tribunals as simply a device used by the Hungarian Communist Party (*Magyar Kommunista Párt*) to seize power and effect elite change. In our study, we were eager to examine whether this was really so and whether the actual data confirm this alleged objective.

The assertions made in this volume are often surprising and contradict what has been claimed previously in the literature. In our view, this reflects the fact that this is the first time that basic research grounded in a comprehensive and methodologically sound approach has been conducted on the topic. In fact, many of our assertions are not so surprising—for instance, our claim that there is a correlation in the justice system between the social status of a defendant and his or her chances of evading punishment and of hiring a paid lawyer. This claim would only be surprising if we—like others in recent years—viewed the people's tribunals as exclusively political in nature rather than as manifestations of a juridical process. In this volume, we have regarded the people's tribunals as instruments in a legal process and have examined their typical features without making any prior political assumptions. Of course, this approach has certain limits, which we analyze in detail in the chapter on methodology. Still, our hope is that the volume will assist in bringing the critical investigation of the history of World War II to a broader audience.

Here we wish to express thanks to all those who have supported our research through their work: Krisztina Czimer, Éva Dani, Fanni Dés, Éva Etelaky †, Nóra Féniász, Júlia Koltai, Zsuzsanna Koltai, Orsolya Kothencz, Anna Sára Ligeti, Hanna Mikes, Melinda Minkó, Ágnes

Néray, Vera Niederfiringer, Mária Szécsényi, Ákos Tasnádi, Álmos Tomasovszky, Éva Vas, and Viola Végh. Special thanks are due to the Rothschild (Europe) Foundation for enabling the realization of our research project, which had been planned for several years.

Political Justice in Europe: The State of Research

Attempting to offer a comparative overview of European judiciary processes between 1944 and 1949 is a challenge. Thus far, this task has been pursued mainly by multi-author volumes, whose introductions tried to set up a taxonomy of European processes (e.g., Deak, Gross, and Judt 2000; for an overview of the process, see Bloxham 2001 and 2004, 397–420; Douglas 2001; Kuretsidis, Haider, and Garscha 1998; Frei, Laak, and Stolleis 2000). The language of sources, the accessibility of sources, and nationally framed memory politics are fundamental issues of European comparative historiography, which define the questions posed.

Literature on post-World War II European judiciary processes confronts methodological and empirical problems as well. Even the various nationally framed comparisons face serious difficulties, given the limits on how much data is accessible or physically manageable for a researcher or group of researchers.

Analysis of early Holocaust resources has recently come into the focus of research, disproving the oversimplifying topos that the given society did not confront the crimes committed on its territory. Court records are such sources. This volume is concerned with Hungarian People's Courts, which are exceptional precisely because of the high number of survivors. In the following, we will offer an overview of the methods used in different countries for analyzing the early court hearings, and the way these relate to the methodological innovation we introduced to the research of the Hungarian administration of political justice.

European research began in the 1990s, and through an analysis of the history of jurisprudence, the establishment of local and national courts has been reconstructed. Among the forerunners of this research were the works of historians in former socialist countries, where anti-fascism used to be the official ideology. Because of them, related publications, though ideologically highly biased, were accessible before the 1990s (e.g., Alexandrov 1969). The first research works examined the "grand trials," the cases of well-known politicians, mainly because the sources for these were well-defined and more easily accessible in the archives. These research works attempted to reconstruct individual court cases based on the court's functioning and the actions of participants.

The second step of the research was to determine numbers: how many courts were involved, and how many convicts were imprisoned or executed, with what kinds of sentences. In the former case, the historians had a relatively easy time setting up the legal framework, because their task was to read the official gazettes. The ministry of justice of the given country prepared the reports, which were often discussed in parliament as well, and thus the records were created. Determining the number of persecuted is a much more difficult task, not only given the uncertainities around post-liberation period's spontaneous lynchings, but also when trying to establish the number of people put on trial. Court sentences were not necessarily carried out: appeals often changed them, and one could ask for clemency. Those sentenced to death were not necessarily executed either. Therefore, the numbers are only estimates, as later micro-researches proved.

After 1989 archival research was allowed in Eastern Europe, and for a short period after 1991, on the territory of the former Soviet Union as well. In the first decade of the 21st century, micro-historical research began, which, based on the sources of regional archives, analyzed the relations of local societies and court hearings (e.g., Olosz 2014; Dimitru 2014, 142–157; Feferman 2003, 587–603). The present volume also contributes to that trend, by using quantitative methodology together with narrative analysis, its primary goal is to offer a complex analysis of processes and to establish causal links.

Among the few comparative works is that of István Deák, who juxtaposed the Austrian and the Hungarian judicial systems from the point of view of the states' respective pasts, using numbers for illustration (Deák 2006, 126–137). In Austria, for political reasons, the rehabilitation of Nazis began in 1948, while in Hungary, partly because of the Soviet occupation, this did not take place. Deák also mentions that Jewish survivors played a crucial role in Hungary but not in Austria. Though former allies of Nazi Germany, both countries quickly denied responsibility—Austria through the myth that it was the "first victim" of Nazi aggression, and Hungary by blaming the Arrow Cross Party and, according to the class-struggle logic, the interwar political elite. Most of the recent Austrian research (Albrich, Garscha, and Polaschek 2006) analyzed surviving court material and established a taxonomy of trials but came to conclusions without any grounding in quantitative research methods.

In Belgium, where, due to the quick liberation process, there was no political vacuum that could have served as a hotbed of atrocities against Jews and civilains, the court was established in 1946. According to Conway's data, which was based on the reports of ministries and parliament records, the courts opened files on 405,067 people with charges of collaboration. Of these, 57,254 were examined, and 2,349 were sentenced to life imprisonment. By 1947 the courts were disbanded, and in the 1950s, those imprisoned were released (Conway 2000, 134). The citizens also participated in the process by flooding the authorities with denunciation letters (Conway 2000, 141). Wouters, in his court-material-based research, pointed out that as early as 1942, Belgium had started to work out the protocol of court hearings, primarily aiming at the Belgian political, economic, and military collaborators—which means that the persecution of Jews was not considered a war crime (Wouters 2010, 222–223). "Ideological collaboration" included participation in the persecution of Jews, but Jews were essentially absent from the process (Wouters 2010, 225). In those parts of Europe that were not occupied by the Soviets, German war criminals were charged with crimes committed in the given country. In Belgium, the Belgian Commission for War Crimes, established December 3, 1944 (Wouters 2010, 233–234), charged 240 Germans. Nineteen were sentenced to death, the rest to life imprisonment.

In Czechoslovakia (Frommer 2005, 96) in May 1947, the prosecution handed over 132,549 cases to the court, but in the end only 38,316 had court hearings, mainly because of a lack of adequate evidence. A total of 14,879 people, primarily of German origin, were expelled from the country. Thirty percent of those who had hearings were acquitted. The deficiency of trained and professionally prepared legal personnel was an issue in Czechoslovakia, just as it was in Hungary (Frommer 2005, 104–105).

In France under the Vichy regime there were three forms of collaboration: ideological, economic, and individual. During the legal processes these were blended together (Rousso 2005, 90). Rousso, based on reports from the Ministry of Justice, determined the numbers from the French political administration of justice: of the files they opened from 311,263 cases, there were 127,751 court hearings, in which 26,361 of the accused were acquitted, 6,763 sentenced to death, 791 executed, 38,266 sentenced to imprisonment or forced labor, and the rest deprived of their political rights (Rousso 2005, 106).

In Greece there was civil war until 1949. The fight against collaborators was framed as the fight against the "enemies of the nation," except that it was not right-wingers getting arrested, like in Soviet-occupied Eastern Europe, but left-wingers (Etmektsoglou 1998, 232). The Legal Prosecution of Collaborators was established May 29, 1944. Under this the hearings of the Greeks who had collaborated with Germans were sluggish, and the high-ranking politicians among them received soft sentences, raising a great deal of public indignation (Etmektsoglou 1998, 241).

By the summer of 1946, of 18,000 collaboration cases, 3,500 were examined. The government went primarily after left-wingers: in 1945 alone, they imprisoned 80,000 people, while from the 16,700 in prison for collaboration, only 2,896 had a court hearing (Etmektsoglou 1998, 251).

In Italy, German atrocities against the partisans were first to make the courts (Battini 2007, 1–25). Putting those Germans on trial who were active on Italian territory fostered the budding myth of the Italian resistance movement and diverted attention from the deeds of the Mussolini regime (Pezzino and Schwarz 2008, 301). Within this framework, Jewish victims were conflated with other victim groups. According to Hans Woller's estimates, between 1945 and 1947, based on the law of April 22, 1945, there were approximately 30,000 court hearings, with thousands of prison sentences and approximately 1,000 death sentences. Just as in France, the trials were extremely short. Nonetheless, most sentences were appealed in the Court of Appeal (Cassazione) and were revoked; only 91 death sentences were implemented. (In France, by contrast, 767 death sentences were implemented and close to 10,500 collaborators were shot immediately after liberation.) In June 1946, when pardon was granted, it was perceived as the "whitewashing of fascist sins." The role of Italians in the deportation and murder of Jews was downplayed (Pezzino and Schwarz 2008, 299–329).

In the Netherlands, preparations for court hearings had begun even during the German occupation of the country. After the liberation,

120,000–150,000 people were placed in internment camps on charges of collaboration. There were 50,000 court hearings, and 152 death sentences were carried out (Romijn 2000, 186–188). Romijn, who analyzed the documents concerning town mayors, established that 950 mayors were investigated and 509 dismissed (Romijn 2000, 189). This is a novel branch of research, which makes claims about political justice based on the screening records of the representatives of authorities, such as mayors and policemen.

One of the first trials took place in Poland, in the fall of 1944, involving a special court. The October 17, 1946, case was taken over by the National Court (Gawron 2010, 285). The Main Commission for Investigation of German Crimes in Poland was established. The first sentence with charges of genocide was also brought in Poland against Goeth (Gawron 2010, 287). The Polish Supreme National Tribunal (NTN) was established in January 1946 to bring major Nazi perpetrators to justice. Between 1946 and 1948, the NTN heard the cases of 49 defendants charged with war crimes and crimes against humanity. The majority of the death camps were on Polish territory, so their commanders were also brought to justice there. In Poland, just as in Hungary, the sentences against the collaborators were issued simultaneously with the ongoing Sovietization of the country, so the trials against the concentration camp guards ran parallel with those against the "obstacles of socialist reconstruction" (Prusin 2010, 1–25).

On the territory of the Soviet Union, the conviction of collaborators and war criminals took place simultaneously with the re-establishment of Soviet power (Hilger, Schmidt, and Wagenlehner 2001). The most immediate targets of retaliation were those who had held positions during the German occupation, but the Soviets also labeled as "collaborators" those opposed to the system (Exeler 2013; Dean 1999; Penter 2005, 782–790; Pastushenko 2013). During the trials held in the Soviet Union, the accused people, under torture, "openly" admitted their wrongdoing (Prusin 2003, 16–17). Feferman analyzed the testimonies collected by the Extraordinary State Commission on Reporting and Investigating the Atrocities of the German Fascist Occupants and their Henchmen and the Damages Inflicted by Them to Citizens, Kolkhozes, Public Organizations, and State Enterprises (Feferman 2003, 587–602). This complicated name indicates that when the main victim groups were defined, the Jews were neglected or treated only one of several groups. For instance in Romania the main aim of the People's Tribunals was to investigate and punish the attrocities agaist the Romanians (Olosz 2014).

The analysis of the methods used in the literature referred to proves that, to make generally applicable statements, a quantitative approach is necessary, involving the systematic research of accessible court materials. Only this approach can guarantee the necessary ground for research based on individual cases. The precondition is the precise assessment of the surviving, accessible documents, and the processes of a national-level political administration of justice, in order to evaluate them. This is the purpose of the next chapter.

Legal Background to the People's Tribunals and Their Operation in Hungary

A significant amount of material is already available on the legal conditions and prerequisites for the operation of the people's tribunals (see Gyenesei 2011). Consequently, this chapter will merely summarize the legal background in order to demonstrate the extent of its fluid nature. It is this fluidity that makes it difficult and even misleading to make claims regarding the "entire process." A certain amount of continuity can be observed in the legal regulation of people's justice: the legal background to the process that some have uniformly called "people's justice" emerged gradually over a period of years. This catchall term is unhelpful because it conceals differences arising in the application of justice during the period. It is also misleading, as judgment was not meted out by "the people" but by members of the political tribunals, who were drawn from the parties of the political elite. The task at hand was to ensure accountability for crimes committed during World War II. Until a proper process could be established—that is, until lawmakers directed their attention to the entire regulatory field—those in charge of the application of the law applied previous laws (laws adopted under the Horthy regime) in the post-World War II justice system.

In Hungary the process of bringing war criminals to justice began with the trial of Reserve Sergeant Péter Rotyits[1] and Reserve Lance Sergeant Sándor Szívós, both of whom had served at the head of Special Labor Battalion no. 401. They were the first put to justice for murdering 124 members of a forced labor unit. The new regime was expressing, tangibly and symbolically, that a new era had begun. The trial of the two men by the newly founded People's Tribunal began on January 31, 1945;

---

1 "I note here that most of the current literature on the subject [...] incorrectly states the name of the reserve sergeant as Rotyis, when in fact it was Rotyits" (Papp 2011, 24). Interestingly, even Ákos Major writes the name as Rotyis (Major, 1988).

death sentences were announced by Council of the People's Judge Ákos Major on February 3. After the Budapest National Committee endorsed the judgment,[2] the sentenced men were publicly executed at Oktogon Square in Budapest on February 4. These were the only executions to be carried out in public. The reaction of people in the crowd led the authorities to perform all subsequent executions in a controlled environment away from public view (for more on this, see Pető 2009c). At the time of these first executions, battles were still raging in the western half of the country. There are several other indications of the authorities' haste: the hanging of the two men took place in extremely primitive conditions; there was no official executioner; and the "rope" used to hang the men consisted of several cords hastily tied together (Major 1988, 125–126). In subsequent trials too, the proper legal background was absent:[3] Prime Ministerial Decree no. 81/1945 (ME) on People's Justice of January 25, 1945 (hereafter PMDPJ) did not enter into force until February 5.

On January 20, 1945, in Moscow, Hungary undertook, in Point 14 of an armistice agreement signed with the Allied Powers, to "cooperate in the apprehension and trial, as well as the surrender to the governments concerned, of persons accused of war crimes." It was to fulfill this obligation that Hungary established its own system of people's tribunals with all its peculiarities: "[The system] was based on a system of lay judges, without, however, returning to [the custom of] trial by jury" (Lukács 1979, 99).

In the literature published before and after 1989, various opinions have been voiced concerning the nature of the people's tribunals. According to Tibor Lukács, the law establishing the system "took the theoretical position that the people's tribunals were extraordinary special courts" (Lukács 1979, 100). While others had argued that the people's tribunals were a delegated forum of international punitive justice, as Hungary was obliged to establish them under the terms of the aforementioned international agreement, Lukács took a different view. He argued that although in establishing a law on people's tribunals, Hungary had indeed been acting to meet

---

2   "The Budapest National Committee was serving both as the court of appeal and as the council of clemency when, on February 3, 1945, it endorsed the original judgment and ordered that the sentence be carried out" (Papp 2011, 29).

3   The judgments were based on the Criminal Code in force (Act V of 1878, also known as the Csemegi Codex). "However, since the new authority, the Budapest National Committee, had declared the prosecution counsel of Dr. Major to be a 'people's court,' we may indeed speak of a people's tribunal case, or of the first trial to be held by the people's tribunal" (Papp 2011, 24).

its international obligations, it was nevertheless "a domestic law of the Hungarian state and would remain so" (Lukács 1979, 291).[4] Unlike Lukács, Attila Papp has argued that "the general framework for, and above all the obligations concerning, people's justice [...] arose from Point 14 of the Armistice Agreement signed in Moscow. [...] in other words, the binding force of an international treaty [...] meant that Hungary was required to proceed against war criminals" (Papp 2011, 46). In Papp's view, a definition formulated in one of the people's tribunal judgments was the most fitting: "A special (exceptional) court established by the law on people's tribunals, a court whose jurisdiction and temporal and territorial scope are determined by new laws, in such a fashion, however, that contrary rules of material law and procedural law have been put aside for the purpose of people's justice while other legal provisions are to be applied in a proper manner" (Papp 2011, 43).

When drafting the PMDPJ, the lawyers tasked with codification had to rely on the building blocks of the existing legal system. These included the Criminal Code (Act V of 1878, sometimes called the Csemegi Codex), the Code of Criminal Procedure (Act XXXIII of 1896), and the Military Criminal Code (Act II of 1930) (Lukács 1979, 95).[5] The text of the PMDPJ also refers to many other laws in force. We found tangible evidence of reliance on existing laws in our investigation of trials held by the people's tribunals. Certain legislative passages were repeatedly cited. Where there were extenuating or mitigating circumstances, reference was usually made to Section 92 of the Criminal Code,[6] while

---

4   Ákos Major took the same position when he wrote: "Our collaboration in holding war criminals to account was based, inter alia, primarily on Hungary's international obligations undertaken in the Armistice Agreement. Yet we also concluded that for this reason, or perhaps in spite of this, we were a Hungarian court and not a justice forum in Hungary of the victorious powers—as I have seen claimed by eminent experts" (Major 1988, 140).

5   A peculiarity of the PMDPJ was that it contained both material legal and procedural legal provisions (Lukács 1979, 283). "Formerly, the course of criminal proceedings—the formalities—had been governed by Act XXXIII of 1896 on criminal procedure and Act XXXIII of 1912 on military criminal procedure, whereas material criminal law had been governed by Act V of 1878 on material criminal law and Act II of 1930 on the Military Criminal Code" (Papp 2011, 14).

6   "If the mitigating circumstances are so consequential and numerous that even the least of the determined punishments would be disproportionately severe, then in such a case the type of crime should be brought down to the lowest degree, and if even this would be too severe, then instead of a prison sentence, one can impose a penitentiary sentence; instead of a penitentiary sentence, a minimum-security-prison sentence; instead of a minimum-security-prison sentence, a monetary fine—to the least degree of these types of punishment. Under the provisions of this section, it is not possible to impose less than 15 years in prison instead of a death sentence, or a smaller punishment of less than 10 years in prison instead of a life prison sentence."

Section 326 of the Code of Criminal Procedure[7] tended to be cited in cases of acquittal. As a result of this trend, we even found interesting cases in which trials were abandoned based on Section 105 of the Criminal Code, which concerned royal pardons.[8]

The decrees and acts of law regulating the system of people's tribunals were subsequently amended on several occasions or supplemented by new ones. The provisional national government's first amendment to the PMDPJ came as early as April 1945 (Prime Ministerial Decree no. 1440/1945 ME—*hereafter the First Amendment to the PMDPJ*). The amendment had retroactive effect—that is to say, it was also to be applied in cases that were ongoing at the time of its entry into force. In August 1945, two additional prime ministerial decrees were issued (Decree no. 5900/1945 ME[9] and Decree no. 6750/1945 ME[10]). In September 1945, the four prime ministerial decrees were transformed into law decrees by Act VII of 1945.[11] Thus until the adoption of Act VII, the people's tribunals and their trials—with all their effects on human lives—were regulated merely at decree level (Karsai 2004, 61).

An extremely important change came with the adoption of Act VII of 1946 on "the protection of the democratic state and the criminal law of the republic." Until this act came into force, the real aim of the system of people's tribunals had been "to punish as soon as possible all

---

7 "An acquittal can be made if 1. the act that forms the subject of the indictment is not a crime, or it is a crime, but a legal judgment in the matter has already been made, 2. the crime forming the basis of the indictment has not been proven, or it is not proven that the defendant committed it, 3. there is a reason that excludes the launching of criminal proceedings or their reliability or punishability, 4. there is a lack of authorization or private or desire motion for legal prosecution, or a revocable motion of a party entitled to launch a private motion has been withdrawn in time."

8 Lukács mentions another example. "Act VII of 1945 [...] also placed under the jurisdiction of the people's tribunals [...] the judgment of various crimes defined in Act III of 1921." This law concerned "the effective defense of the governmental and social order" and served after the defeat of the Republic of Councils (the short-lived communist regime of 1919) to enable the punishment of those who had participated in it (Lukács 1979, 101). In our sample, we found three cases where the provisions of this law were cited as the basis for the indictments. The crimes alleged in the indictments were "dishonoring the Hungarian state" (Section 7 of Act III of 1921) (Budapest City Archives [BCA] 603/1949), "defaming the nation" (Section 7 of Act III of 1921) (BCA 3426/1946), and "bringing shame on the nation" (Section 8 of Act III of 1921) (BCA 504/1949).

9 Prime Ministerial Decree on the rules to be applied in proceedings against absent indicted persons and the representation of the public prosecution. The decree "established the institution of the public accuser alongside that of the public (people's) prosecutor. The people's accuser functioned outside the organization of the public prosecutor's office but had the same rights as the public prosecutor." (Papp 2011, 57)

10 Prime Ministerial Decree on improving the work discipline of public officials.

11 "By means of a peculiar codification technique, the act did not place the basic decree in a uniform structure with the recent amendments and supplements. Rather, the various parts were raised to the level of a law in separation, as appendices I–IV of Act VII of 1945" (Papp 2011, 19–20).

those who had caused or participated in the historical disaster suffered by the Hungarian people" (preamble to the PMDPJ). Act VII of 1946, however, provided for the creation of special councils at the people's tribunals, and these special councils "increasingly became a device for the Hungarian Communist Party (*Magyar Kommunista Párt*) to engage and suppress their political opponents" (Papp 2011, 38–39). Indeed, Act VII empowered the people's tribunals to issue judgments concerning acts committed after the war, and this change fundamentally altered the public view of wartime crimes and the entire justice process. This action caused the period between 1945 and 1946 to fall into oblivion by conflating it with the period after 1946 (for a similar periodization, see Karsai 2000, 233–252).

Further significant changes took place with the adoption of Act XXXIV of 1947, which not only amended the prime ministerial decrees raised into law decrees by Act VII of 1945 but also included provisions supplementing the contents of Act VII of 1946.

The System of People's Tribunals and the Actors in the Process

The PMDPJ ordered the establishment of people's tribunals at all courts of justice (Section 37 of the PMDPJ). This resulted in the creation of 24 people's tribunals between January and May 1945 (Papp 2011, 33). Several councils (or divisions) could operate within a single people's tribunal. It is thought that there were 50–60 people's tribunal councils in all of Hungary. The Budapest People's Tribunal began its work on March 6, 1945[12] (Papp 2011, 33).

A people's tribunal council had five members (people's judges), who were delegated by the five political parties constituting the Hungarian National Independence Front[13] (Section 39 of the PMDPJ). In a legal sense, the people's judges were lay judges. Under the First Amendment to the PMDPJ, the number of members of a people's tribunal council was increased to six: in addition to the members delegated by the parties, a

---

12 According to documents at the Budapest City Archives, the Budapest People's Tribunal began operating on February 28, 1945. http://bfl.archivportal.hu/id-1160-nepbirosagok.html (accessed August 23, 2012).
13 The Democratic Citizens Party *(Demokratikus Polgári Párt)*, the Independent Smallholders Party *(Független Kisgazda Párt)*, the Hungarian Communist Party *(Magyar Kommunista Párt)*, the National Peasants Party *(Nemzeti Parasztpárt)*, and the Social Democratic Party *(Szociáldemokrata Párt)*.

member was sent by the National Trade Union Council (*Országos Szakszervezeti Tanács*) (Section 19 of the First Amendment to the PMDPJ).

A professional judge was assigned to each people's tribunal council (Section 42 of the PMDPJ) as its head, but since such judges were not given voting rights, they were not real members of the people's tribunal councils (Papp 2011, 60). The task of a head judge was to assist the lay members of the people's tribunal council in making a proper judgment by "summarizing the result of the trial and offering professional information on the applicable laws and decrees and on the type and degree of sentence to be issued" and by "giving an opinion, based on the evidence provided in the course of the trial, as to what crime may have been committed" (Section 49 of the PMDPJ). The law also emphasized, however, that a head judge was to merely outline the various options and to refrain from telling members of the council how he might have decided (Section 49 of the PMDPJ). Judgments were decided in votes by the council, whereby the head judge was not entitled to vote.[14] The rules pertaining to the head judges were changed somewhat by the First Amendment to the PMDPJ, which stated that "the head judge can only voice an opinion (not in every case) on the proven nature of a criminal act if he is requested to do so by at least one member of the council" (Section 20 of the First Amendment to the PMDPJ). Moreover, the head judge could subsequently vote in cases where there was a tie vote (Section 20 of the First Amendment to the PMDPJ). After a council had passed judgment, it was the task of the head judge to draft a sentence (Section 49 of the PMDPJ). In this respect, the PMDPJ authorized the head judge, in cases where a sentence could not be appealed or where the right to appeal had not been exercised (Lukács 1979, 306), to "submit in a closed envelope a petition to the National Council of People's Tribunals on behalf of the defendant, if it is his belief that the decision of the people's judges has violated essential measures of this present decree" (Section 50 of the PMDPJ). In such cases, the head judge was not to in-

---

14 The only exception was when the lay members of the Council were unable to reach a decision. At such times the head judge could add his vote to two other concurring votes (Section 49 of the PMDPJ). "The decision-making process, in which each member had equal rights, consisted of two stages. In the first stage, a decision was taken (by simple majority) on the question of guilt and—if the accused was guilty—on the exact crime for which he was to be punished. Where a defendant was guilty, a decision was taken in the second stage (once again by simple majority) on the sanction to be applied against him. Under the decree, it was obligatory that the most senior people's judge should begin the voting and that the youngest should conclude it" (Papp 2011, 62).

form members of the council of his action, and the submission of a petition had no suspensory effect (Section 50 of the PMDPJ). "[Such] a petition by the head judge constituted a special legal remedy" (Lukács 1979, 305).

The special councils established under Act VII of 1946 differed slightly in terms of their composition: the Civil Democratic Party (*Polgári Demokrata Párt*) no longer delegated a member (Section 11 of Act VII of 1946).[15]

A major change in the composition of the people's tribunal councils took effect January 1, 1948, with the entry into force of Act XXXIV of 1947 *(hereafter the Second Amendment to the PMDPJ)*. The people's tribunal councils once again had five members, but the composition was different: the trade unions and the Civil Democratic Party (*Polgári Demokrata Párt*) were no longer entitled to send delegates to the councils, and the head judges became full voting members[16] (Section 12 of the Second Amendment to the PMDPJ).

In trials held by the people's tribunals, public prosecutors were responsible for pressing charges. The public prosecutors were legal professionals appointed by the minister of justice (Section 24 of the PMDPJ). In addition, there were also lay prosecutors, known as political prosecutors. "The powers of the political prosecutors were not regulated by law; rather, they were shaped by practice. Their legal status corresponded with that of the aggrieved party, as they represented the universal aggrieved party, the Hungarian people [...]. The public prosecutor exercised rights pertaining to the indictment, while the political prosecutor, since there was no prosecutor's office, was due the rights generally enjoyed by an aggrieved party" (Papp 2011, 57).

At the people's tribunals, defendants were also defended by lawyers: under Section 36 of the PMDPJ, the provisions of Chapter V of the Code of Criminal Procedure relating to the defense of defendants were to be applied. However, one should note—and we shall return to this later on—that the defense had limited rights: "It was not independent;

---

15 Importantly, however, the delegate remained a member of the National Council of People's Tribunals.
16 The Second Amendment to the PMDPJ clarified the issue of the head judge's right to vote by stating that he had to vote after the people's judges (Section 16 of the Second Amendment to the PMDPJ). Moreover, from then on the head judge's right of submission was abolished—which had been contained in Section 50 of the PMDPJ.

it could only act using powers that were also due to defendants"[17] (Lukács 1979, 312).

The National Council of People's Tribunals reviewed judgments of the people's tribunals that had been appealed (Section 56 of the PMDPJ). The National Council consisted of five-member councils, once again comprising delegates from the five political parties in the Hungarian National Independence Front.[18] However, those delegated to the National Council were required to be professional judges with judicial or legal qualifications (Section 57 of the PMDPJ). When the number of members of the people's tribunals was altered by the First Amendment to the PMDPJ, the number of members of the National Council did not change. The National Trade Union Council (*Országos Szakszervezeti Tanács*) was not entitled to delegate a member. The Second Amendment to the PMDPJ changed the number and composition of members of the National Council in line with the people's tribunal councils (Section 14 of the Second Amendment to the PMDPJ). At the National Council of People's Tribunals, the chief public prosecutor pressed charges against defendants (Section 54 of the PMDPJ).

"To ensure the standardization of sentencing practice," notes Lukács, "there was a need for the National Council of People's Tribunals to take decisions that provided guidance on theoretical, legal policy and interpretative issues, whereby lower courts, having acquainted themselves with such decisions, could then follow them in their sentencing practice" (Lukács 1979, 349). Thus the National Council, in addition to its functions as stipulated by law (Section 56 of the PMDPJ), "became the guide for sentencing practice" (Lukács 1979, 350). The National Council's assumption of this role also reflected Section 22 of the Second Amendment to the PMDPJ, which introduced to the law governing the people's tribunals the possibility of legal remedy[19] (for the sake of the standard uniformity of the law) when it declared that "the chief public

---

17 This was much more restricted than in today's legal system, because under the current system "the defense attorney takes part in the procedure by his own right; his duties and rights are independent of the duties, entitlements, and rights of the defendant. There is only one limit to his powers: he cannot do anything that would be prejudicial to or against the interests of his client" (Lukács 1979, 311).

18 The Democratic Citizens Party *(Demokratikus Polgári Párt)*, the Independent Smallholders Party *(Független Kisgazda Párt)*, the Hungarian Communist Party *(Magyar Kommunista Párt)*, the National Peasants Party *(Nemzeti Parasztpárt)*, and the Social Democratic Party *(Szociáldemokrata Párt)*.

19 The institution of legal remedy was already known in Hungarian criminal law; it was governed by Section 441 of the Code of Criminal Procedure. The influence of earlier legislation is indicated by the fact that the text of the new regulation was clearly based on the previous law.

prosecutor can exercise legal remedy at the National Council of the People's Tribunals against any final decision or other measure of a people's tribunal […] which is in breach of a law." In such cases, the legal uniformity council of the National Council of the People's Tribunals was to proceed, and this legal uniformity council was to be headed by the chairman of the National Council of the People's Tribunals.

The Crimes and the Range of Punishments

The PMDPJ "established the concept of war crimes and crimes against the people and defined their statutory basis"[20] (Lukács 1979, 96). The term "political criminal act" was given a new interpretation in the decree: "Section 20 of the PMDPJ placed the judgment of crimes committed in connection with war crimes and crimes against the people and other crimes listed in the legal provision[21] under the jurisdiction of the people's tribunals" (Lukács 1979, 233). We should also note that, regarding these crimes, the people's tribunals had jurisdiction if a criminal act had been political in nature (Section 21 of the PMDPJ). Section 3 of the PMDPJ listed the range of applicable punishments. They were as follows: death, maximum-security prison, penitentiary, internment, a monetary fine up to and including the confiscation of assets, loss of job or ban on exercising one's profession, suspension of political rights, and several other disciplinary sanctions.[22] All of these punishments could be imposed as the primary punishment, while the latter three could also be imposed as secondary punishments, sometimes to be determined cumulatively. Compared to the previous punishment categories,[23] the most significant change was the inclusion of internment—even if this was to last only for a short time.[24] Section 3 of the First Amendment to the PMDPJ altered the system of punishments. Consequently, the range of

---

20 The provisions placed war criminals in five separate groups (see Papp 2011, 13).
21 Such crimes included espionage, arson, the violation of public health rules, and the destruction of property.
22 When defining the various crimes, Section 3 of the PMDPJ referred to Prime Ministerial Decree no. 15 of 1945, which concerned the identification of public employees and authorized the people's tribunals to impose the punishments listed there. These were public reprimand, redeployment, a pronouncement that the person was unfit to fill a senior position, and a ban on promotion for one to five years.
23 These were contained in Sections 20 and 53 of the Criminal Code.
24 It also removed the state minimum-security prison.

punishments now included forced labor and the complete or partial confiscation of assets, but internment,[25] penitentiary sentences, and disciplinary sanctions were removed from among the available options. In addition, a strict distinction was made between primary[26] and secondary punishments.[27] The latter could be applied even when they were not required under the legal provision relating to the particular crime. Moreover, the First Amendment to the PMDPJ mandated the suspension of political rights whenever a defendant was found guilty.

Sections 11–18 of the PMDPJ contained provisions governing the establishment of crimes and the maximum punishments for such crimes. The crimes referred to in these paragraphs were "liable to prosecution" (Section 19 of the PMDPJ), which meant that the authorities were required to proceed whenever such matters were brought to their attention. The First Amendment to the PMDPJ expanded the range of war crimes and crimes against the people.

It is crucial to note that when determining the jurisdiction of the people's tribunals, lawmakers based their approach on the type of crime committed rather than on the person committing the crime. Section 20 of the PMDPJ determined the range of crimes that could only be judged by the people's tribunals. Meanwhile, Section 2 stated that "the jurisdiction of the people's tribunals extends to civilian individuals and members of the armed forces,[28] including the police force and the gendarmerie, as well as any individuals captured on the territory of the Hungarian state or extradited to the Hungarian state, regardless of their citizenship." Section 6 of the PMDPJ stated, furthermore, that "criminal indictments may also be pursued against fugitive accused persons."

Act VII of 1946 expanded the range of crimes that were to be judged by the special councils established within the people's tribunals. This

---

25 The reason was that, with the formation of a new police force, this punishment now fell under the jurisdiction of the police (Lukács 1979, 434–435).
26 These were death, forced labor, penitentiary, and prison.
27 These were monetary fine, confiscation of assets, loss of job or ban on exercising profession, and the suspension of political rights.
28 Under the laws in force, where a crime had been committed by a soldier, a military court had jurisdiction. "Here there is tangible evidence of the mentality of the legislator that war crimes and crimes against the people are special offenses, and that as such a special judicial body should judge the criminal." It is evident, therefore, that "the legislator assigned the court not on the basis of the person committing the act but according to the crimes committed by that person" (Papp 2011, 70). The legality of this was disputed: the minister of defense tried repeatedly to ensure that soldiers would be tried in military courts or at least that the investigation (of their crimes) would be conducted by military investigative bodies (Lukács 1979, 407–409; Papp 2011, 70–73).

change enabled the regime to eliminate its real and perceived opponents. "From the outset, the variably interpretable terminology—such as association, movement, incitement and so forth—and intentional verbosity of this act of law, which abrogated provisions relating to political crimes and introduced new notions of crime, meant that [...] it could be implemented based on whatever was the prevailing political judgment" (Szakács and Zinner 1997, 195). The categories of crime remained unchanged, but where a crime mentioned in the legislation was committed and a defendant found guilty, there was now a requirement to impose, as a secondary punishment, the suspension of political rights coupled with the loss of public office as well as the partial or full confiscation of assets. The same section of the act also provided that "in instances of crime, a foreigner must be deported from the country and a permanent prohibition placed on his return, while a domestic citizen must be banished from the locality where his or her residence represents a threat to the democratic state, even if this is the official place of residence of the convicted" (Section 10 of Act VII of 1946).

Controversies Surrounding the Law on People's Tribunals

The law governing the people's tribunals dealt with certain issues differently from the other laws in force. As a result, disputes arose rather frequently. In what follows, we present some of these legal issues, which inevitably tended to be interpreted by contemporary legal experts and politicians in line with their party allegiances.

In order to ensure retroactive punishment, the law governing the people's tribunals violated two classical principles of law:[29] *nullum crimen sine lege*[30] and *nulla poena sine lege*.[31] Section 1 of the PMDPJ stipulated that "the crimes described in this decree shall be punishable where the criminal act has [already] been perpetrated on entry into force of this decree, and was not punishable under the legal provisions in force at the time of the perpetration of the criminal act."

---

29 The suspension of these legal principles was in line with European practice at the time (Karsai 2004, 61–62; Lukács 1979, 208–209).
30 This means "no crime without law." It is the principle in criminal law that a person cannot face criminal punishment except for an act that was criminalized by law before he or she performed the act.
31 This means "no penalty without law." It is the principle that a person cannot be punished for doing something that is not prohibited by law.

The law governing the people's tribunals altered the criminal liability (and punishability) of minors. Section 22 of the PMDPJ provided that a people's tribunal could proceed in matters involving minors and could impose on those aged over 15 years any punishment contained in the decree, with the exception of the death sentence. Under Section 15 of the First Amendment to the PMDPJ, any punishment could be imposed on a person aged over 15 years at the time of the crime, while persons aged over 16—unlike before—could be sentenced to death. Monetary fines, the confiscation of assets, the loss of a job, or a ban on exercising one's profession were punishments that could be imposed without regard to the age of the convicted person.

Another problem area was the introduction of restrictions on a person's right to appeal. This represented a significant breach of the principle of the equal treatment of clients, "for the party pressing charges [the prosecutor] had a broader range of rights than the defendant or the lawyer acting on his or her behalf" (Lukács 1979, 312). Only in the case of a severe sentence[32] imposed for a crime defined in the law could a convicted defendant appeal to the National Council of the People's Tribunals, but—as already noted—his or her defense lawyer did not have the right to appeal. Meanwhile, however, public prosecutors could launch appeals whenever they wanted—whether to get the sentence reduced or increased. They could also lodge objections to appeals made by defendants (Section 53 of the PMDPJ). According to the First Amendment to the PMDPJ, a public prosecutor could only appeal a decision in order to achieve a stiffer sentence, but in the course of such an appeal, the judgment could also be altered, under certain circumstances, to the advantage of the convicted defendant. The right of appeal of a convicted defendant was, however, made subject to further restrictions: the right of appeal was removed in cases involving the gravest crimes, while in other cases it was limited. Under the First Amendment to the PMDPJ, a defense lawyer still had no separate right of appeal. Indeed, a further restriction was introduced: the defense lawyer could only lodge an appeal if a defendant gave his or her consent (Section 21 of the First Amendment to the PMDPJ). The Second Amendment to the PMDPJ introduced further restrictions: it abrogated the sections of the PMDPJ and the Amend-

---

32 These were the following: death penalty, full confiscation of assets or loss of one's job, a three-year prison sentence, and a fine in excess of 20,000 pengős.

ment to the PMDPJ providing for appeals and replaced the institution of appeal with a "complaint of annulity." Such a complaint, however, could only be submitted in cases where there had been a significant breach of the provisions of the law. A complaint of annulity was not permitted on a point of fact (Section 19 of the Second Amendment to the PMDPJ).

Two additional factors should be considered when evaluating the law on people's tribunals. In the literature, trials held by the people's tribunals are portrayed as political trials. Political trials were "political" either because the subject matter was a crime or conspiracy against the state or because the investigation was politically motivated. A trial could also be political because its aim was not only legal but also political in a direct sense. It is possible to distinguish between the different types of political trial, doing so—according to Christenson—on the basis of whether the law was being used merely as an alibi (as, for instance, in the Rajk trial[33]) or the court was truly operating on a legal basis and within a legal framework, as was claimed by the people's tribunals (Christenson 1986, 10–11). It is worth noting that the Hungarian state established after 1945 was an activist state; one of its clear objectives was that criminal cases should not only settle legal disputes but also serve state objectives (see Damaska 1986). Seen in this light, all trials held by the people's tribunals were necessarily political trials; they were based on the same elements, concepts, and procedures as Hungary's pre-1945 jurisdiction and so fit into the Hungarian legal milieu.[34]

The second factor is the establishment of what amounted to a new and parallel court structure. The newly established people's tribunals were lay courts, which had, so to speak, no tradition in Hungarian law. However, jury courts had existed in Hungary until 1914 and so were part of the Hungarian tradition.

In this chapter we have discussed the legal framework surrounding the justice system in the aftermath of World War II. In the next chapter we examine how one can analyze the process outside a historical legal framework, thus going beyond changes in the law.

---

33 The first Stalinist show trial in Hungary was held in 1949 which ended with executing László Rajk (1909-1949) on 15 October, 1949 as an alleged spy for Yugoslavia. Ha was rehabilitated in 1955 and reburied on 6 October, 1956 which was the first mass demonstration against the communist regime in Hungary.
34 As we have shown in this chapter, in the course of the history of the legal development of the law on people's tribunals, a relatively flexible framework gradually became regulated in ever-greater detail: Act VII of 1945 supplemented the provisions of numerous government decrees, while Act XXXIV of 1947 summarized the earlier changes.

Research Methodology

The purpose of our research has been to map out and evaluate the system of people's tribunals after World War II and to reveal how the trials ran their course and who participated in them. Previous research projects had been conducted at two levels:[35] either the researchers examined the institutional network or they described individual cases. Such a methodology could not give us a comprehensive and valid picture of all the case files.

The innovation in our research is the methodology we used to approach the topic. On the one hand, the case files were examined through quantitative social research; on the other hand, the results were both quantified and generalized. This chapter deals with the difficulties and methodology of the research.

Method of Approach

There are basically two approaches to empirical research: explorative and confirmative. In explorative research the researcher does not have any hypotheses; rather, the aim is to widen and deepen knowledge of a given area that is usually underexplored. Conclusions are drawn on the basis of the newly acquired data. In confirmative research, hypotheses are tested. In our research these two approaches were applied concurrently. Concerning the confirmative approach, we used the existing data to establish hypotheses we wished to test. However, explorative data collection was also very important, since, owing to the lack of pre-

---

35 A partial exception is, for instance, the research conducted by László Karsai (2004), which we also mention in the chapter "Jewish Identity and the People's Tribunals."

vious systematic research, we did not know what data were to be found. With this assumption as our starting point, we collected all the data in the case files that met certain criteria (described later on). The aim was the structuralized exploration of the case files created by the people's tribunals.

As already noted, with regard to the findings, the aim was twofold: the quantification and generalization of the collected data. It will be shown that these two aspects are interdependent: to put it simply, quantification is one means by which a generalization can be reached. It is important to mention this point, as this formed the basis for our research design (the research plan).

Quantitative social research, as its name implies, works with numbers. Thus the first task was to encode the information contained in the people's tribunal case files. This required us to determine what information was retrievable from the files. Some pieces of information could be retrieved from the files directly, while others were accessible only indirectly. One example of the former was the records/minutes in the files that included questionnaires with the socio-demographic data of defendants. However, even the direct data were not always in the same place in the case files; sometimes, in order to retrieve the required information, one had to read a complete case file. We also came across information that was only indirectly referenced. One example of this is whether a case involved Jews. All this demonstrates the important role played by those colleagues[36] who were responsible for collecting the data in our research project.

There were other criteria that the data had to match. Quantitative analysis is not suitable for examining "the individual." Consequently, when exploring the files, we were looking for similarities; that is to say, we searched for data that might be found in every file. Some information that originally met these criteria turned out later to be so incomplete that it was not worth collecting.

It should also be borne in mind that if one decides against examining particularity, then this inevitably results in some information loss. On the other hand, quantitative research compensates for such loss by affording generalization. In other words, based on the sample surveyed, one can draw general conclusions for the whole pool of data. For this to

---

36 We refer to them throughout the book as encoders, even though they also recorded information and data.

be possible, in our case the sample had to be representative of all case files. Thus we required an appropriate sampling method. The details of our sampling method are described in detail below.

Preparation Phase

As we prepared for the research, we looked first at one of the larger and more detailed case files. Based on the contents of this "exemplary" case file and on what we already knew from the literature, we selected those primary data items that we supposed would be present in each case file. At this stage, we focused on the basic data contained in the case files (e.g., the start date and completion date of the legal cases), as well as the "questionnaires" found in the case files. On this basis the primary questionnaire used during the pilot stage of our research was compiled.

Pilot research

The pilot research had three goals: (1) to compile the content of the final questionnaire; (2) to finalize the structure of the questionnaire; and (3) to define the method of research. At this stage, 20 case files were selected, so that each surveyed year would be represented. It was supposed that the case files from different years might differ from each other. Thus it was crucial that the pilot questionnaire and the research method would be suitable for all case files.

On the basis of the results of the pilot research, the questionnaire was continuously modified and the final version compiled. Basically, three major changes were made: (1) the questions and the encoding methods were changed; (2) it was decided that new data should also be recorded; (3) data earlier thought to have been relevant were omitted as being irrelevant or sporadic. It was at this stage of research that the possible attributes of certain variables (answers to questions) were finalized. Our main aim was to establish possible answers in advance—that is, to make use of as many "closed" questions as possible. Sometimes, however, this method could only be used in part or not at all. In the former case, a mixed recording system was used. For instance, if a defendant had been a member of a party or organization, but these were not named, the encoders were asked to record the answers word for word. There were questions where closed answers simply could not be used—for example, questions concerning the place of birth and occupation of a defendant or witness.

The final structure of the questionnaire was mostly influenced by the content of the case files, so a flexible questionnaire was needed. It was important to address the fact that, for instance, certain cases had multiple defendant and multiple witnesses, because then their data had to be recorded more than once. Therefore the questionnaire was divided into two parts: a constant part and a variable part. The basic data retrieved from the case files were recorded in the constant part, whereas data concerning the defendants, lawyers, crimes committed, trials, sentences, and witnesses featured in the variable part.

As already noted, research method was finalized during the pilot stage. The aim was to ensure that the process of collecting and encoding data was as unambiguous as possible. One characteristic feature of quantitative measurement is its reliability, meaning that the first measurement and subsequent measurements give similar results. In our case, reliability implied that when the same case file was given to different encoders, the results should be very similar. Therefore it was vital to formulate the questions and answer-categories in such a way that they would mean the same thing to each encoder. Sometimes supplementary explanations were given to clarify what certain data meant. To cite a very simple example, the encoders had to record when a certain legal case started. By our definition the start date was the earliest date found in the documents of a given case file. There were also instances when one piece of data occurred in several different forms. In such instances it was crucial to define exactly how to record the data. For example, where a defendant's name had different spellings, we specified that the version featuring in his or her signature was to be regarded as authentic. If this proved unsatisfactory, then the incidence rate was taken into account, and where this failed, all spellings were recorded.

Expert roundtable

At this stage in the research, we held a roundtable discussion attended by experts in various academic fields.[37] We first sent them some prelim-

---

[37] The experts attending the roundtable discussion were Károly Bárd, László Csősz, Gábor Kádár, András Kovács, and Antal Örkény. We are thankful for their helpful advice.

inary discussion material about the research. The discussion began with a general introduction to the research project, followed by a detailed description of our methodology. We asked the experts to tell us what they thought about the research. We were also able to question them on issues arising during the first phase of the research.

It is worth highlighting two important outcomes of the roundtable discussion. First, at several points we added new questions to the questionnaire. Second, we broadened the research methods somewhat: to enhance our understanding, we integrated qualitative elements into what had originally been conceived as exclusively quantitative research. Consequently, both before and after the research, we held interviews with the encoders. Prior to the research we asked them about their knowledge of the people's tribunals and their expectations concerning the project. Then, on completion of the project, we questioned them about their experiences. The aim of all this was both to prepare them for the difficult and emotionally draining work in the archives and to give them the feeling of being real partners in the project. During the conversations, it became apparent how little the encoders knew about post-World War II Hungarian history, even though they were students at a top university in Budapest. Most of their knowledge came from family stories and historical films; what they knew depended to a great extent on their family background. These interviews proved to us that it was correct to pay attention to the feelings and anxieties of the encoders, as the project's success required good relations between the assistant researchers and the head researchers. Given that each encoder had to work in the archives for several months, the reliability of the research depended on their conscientiousness and diligence.

For each case file, the encoders were asked to make a sound file, containing a brief statement on the topic of the case file, as well as anything else they deemed interesting or important. These recordings greatly assisted our research. First, they were of assistance when decisions had to be made in disputed or problematic areas. Second, they deepened our understanding by providing us with the stories behind the raw data.

Training of the Encoders

As our research did not involve a traditional questionnaire survey, we had to pay special attention to the selection and training of the encoders.[38] During the first briefing, their tasks were explained in detail, while the structure and filling in of the questionnaire was mentioned in general terms. We went through the questionnaire item by item. Where something was not clear, we talked it through or tackled the issue by correcting the previous manual. The next step in the training process was a visit to the archive, where the encoders met the archivists and were able to see some case files.

One medium-sized case file encoded during the pilot research phase was selected for a test-run of the questionnaire. As the next step in the training process, we asked the encoders to do a test-run on this case file. Each encoder was given a copy of the case file, the questionnaire, and a manual for filling in the questionnaire. They were asked not only to encode the case file but also to note all their questions and comments. The encoding test-run had two aims: first, to give the encoders some experience encoding the data; second, to test the reliability of our questionnaire. It was now possible to compare the questionnaires filled in by the encoders with the results we had found during the pilot research. We could also compare how the encoders had filled in the questionnaires. Questions that were found to be ambiguous were modified.

The Final Questionnaire

The final questionnaire consisted of eight data sheets. In the following, we indicate how often each sheet had to be filled in and what data were encoded.
- Data sheet of the case file: filled in once.
  - *Content of the data sheet: number of used data sheets; data concerning the content of the case file (for example, whether the case file contained the criminal charges, the court report, etc.)*

---

38 In a traditional research survey, they would be the interviewers.

- Data sheet of the data of the case: filled in once.
  - *Content of the data sheet: the beginning and the end of the case; number of hearings; possible delays; whether it concerned Jews and/or communists; whether there was a rehearing after 1950.*
- Data sheet of the defendant: filled in according to the number of defendants.
  - *Content of the data sheet: socio-demographic data of defendants; membership (party, organization), previous punishment(s) (if any).*
- Data sheet of the lawyer: filled in according to the number of defendants.
  - *Content of the data sheet: name of the lawyer; beginning of his/her assignment; whether he/she was court-appointed or paid.*
- Data sheet of the indictment: filled in according to the number of defendants and of the levels in the case.
  - *Content of the data sheet: lawsuit place of the indictment (charges); type of charges.*
- Data sheet of the hearings: filled in according to the number of hearings.
  - *Content of the data sheet: date of the hearings, name of the judge; data of the tribunals; whether the accused was present at the hearing.*
- Data sheet of the sentence: filled in according to the number of defendants and the levels in the case.
  - *Content of the data sheet: the basis of the sentence; if the defendant was sentenced, the punishment; if the defendant was acquitted, the basis for the acquittal; if the accused was sentenced to death, whether he/she was pardoned by the president; whether there was an appeal.*
- Data sheet of the witnesses: filled in according to the number of witnesses.
  - *Content of the data sheet: socio-demographic data of the witness; membership (party, organization); relation to the defendant; whether he/she suffered any damage during the case.*

Research Phase

The first step in the research project was to select an appropriate sample. In the course of our research, we examined 500 of 22,000 case files created by the Budapest People's Tribunal.

Sampling procedure

In accordance with the basic aim of quantitative research, our aim was to gain information about all the files[39] based on a sample. In other words, we sought to obtain results that could be generalized. To achieve this aim, we needed to ensure that the selected case files were representative of all case files. Thus an appropriate probability sampling method was required.

As already noted, our initial hypothesis stated—and it was confirmed by the pilot research—that there were significant differences among the lawsuits depending on the year in which they were held. Our aim was to analyze the data for the entire period and for each year separately. This meant we needed a sufficient amount of data. We decided to select 100 case files from each year, even though we knew that the trials were not evenly distributed among the various years. Thus each case file in a given year had the same chance of being included in the sample. This was done by random number generator; that is, the case files were chosen randomly by using their numbers. This procedure is called stratified random sampling.

Based on the research, we could venture to make statements concerning the entire surviving documentary material of the Budapest People's Tribunal through our analysis of only 500 case files. Since the sample was taken exclusively from the files of the Budapest People's Tribunal, our findings can only be extrapolated for this population (i.e., for cases in Budapest).

From filling in the questionnaires to the data files

After completion of the aforementioned steps, we were able to begin screening the files selected through sampling. At this stage of the research, we encountered for the first time the problem of the "quality" of the data. In the classic case, data "arise" after the research framework (e.g., a questionnaire) has been established. When mapping a legal procedure, however, this all takes place in reverse: the data already exist, and a system has to be established that accommodates these data and facilitates an investigation of their general features. The system is created,

---

39 By all case files we mean the surviving documentation held at the Budapest City Archives.

however, before there is a deep understanding of the data, and this is true despite the pilot phase.

Data under investigation may be static or dynamic. For data to be static, there must be some permanent feature or characteristic. Here the essential point, as noted above, is that there should be quantifiable and accessible data for a large number of cases. Meanwhile, dynamic data refer to processes or data that indicate the various stages in a procedure and which we record in order to draw conclusions about the course of such procedures. Quantitative research can be employed only where a process has a strict internal logic, where the rules of the procedure are fixed, and where deviation from such rules is typical in only a negligible percentage of cases.

In our research, we were working with both static and dynamic data. Static data included, for instance, data relating to the beginning and end of a trial or the socio-demographic features of defendants and witnesses. Dynamic data, meanwhile, were those relating to the course of the procedure: the triad of indictment, judgment, and sentence. Here it is important that there be a close logical relationship between the various elements.

Concerning the static data, our task was simply—although this was not always so simple—to measure the range of data accessible to us from the case files of the people's tribunals. In the case of dynamic data, in view of the formal nature of the legal system, we assumed that the processes underway at the people's tribunals met the requirements for dynamic data described above. We thought, therefore, that the data were in order and that this order was governed by the decrees and laws adopted in connection with the people's tribunals. However, a systematic investigation of the case files revealed that, unfortunately, the supposed order did not exist in the files.[40] The first finding of the research was therefore that when studying such legal processes, we should only apply quantitative research in a limited manner. Consequently, the qualitative elements in the research assumed greater importance as the data were being processed.

Once all the selected files had been examined, questionnaires were filled in. The next task was to create a data file suitable for the statistical

---

[40] A varying quality of data and frequent omissions and inaccuracies were also encountered by László Karsai during his research (Karsai 2004, 69).

software. First, a data frame file was created using the spreadsheet application Excel. All data of a given file were put into one column, and all the answers given to one certain question (i.e., the gender of the first defendant) were put into one row.[41] If a data sheet was filled in more than once, this was recorded accordingly in the frame file. As an indication of the extent of the data, it is worth noting that after the summation of all data sheets, the unified Excel files contained 7,700 rows. Evidently, there was no database with a piece of data for each cells in the Excel file, but in order for us to create a data file with 500 case files from the databases of the various encoders, it was necessary for each data file to have the same structure. That is to say, given that there was, for example, one case with 13 defendants, the frame file had to be capable of recording a data sheet for 13 defendants, regardless of the fact that in most cases there was only a single defendant.

It was imperative that encoders use a standardized encoding method when recording the answers. Therefore they were given a detailed recording manual where the recording method for each and every question was defined. During the recording procedure, the attributes were retained, as noted above. Where possible they were recorded using numbers; where verbal answers were needed, the answers were recorded using text.

First each encoder recorded the questionnaires of two case files. They were asked to note all their problems and questions. These were discussed individually, after which the final instructions for recording were compiled. Subsequently, the recording of the data of the 500 files began.

After the completion of the Excel files, the data were formulated so that they would be compatible with the chosen statistical software. In this program the rows of the data files contained the cases, while the columns contained the variables. Thus the data had to be "turned around," which, since each encoder had a table with 7,700 rows and 50 columns[42] (i.e., 385,000 cells), was no easy task and resulted in many technical problems, all of which had to be resolved.

Statistical programs deal with numbers, and so the already recorded verbal variables had to be encoded into numbers in order to produce the final data file. Here we had to accomplish several different tasks. The

---

[41] Since the reverse is true in the case of the statistical software package, it would theoretically have been logical to proceed in this manner at this point, but there were technical obstacles to this.
[42] Each of the 10 encoders recorded the data for 50 case files.

simplest—although this, too, was very time-consuming—was to assign a code to the various political parties and organizations. Here we "merely" had to collect all the various parties and organizations and assign them each a code in order to facilitate processing. A more complex procedure was assigning a code to the various courts of law. For the indictments, the data included, in theory, the relevant provision of law (e.g., Point 3 of Section 11 of the PMDPJ) and the named category of crime (e.g., war crime). In the case of the judgments, the only piece of data was the relevant provision of law. However, we encountered significant variation in how these data were shown, and yet we knew that the data had to look the same in order for the statistical software to view it as identical—this was a prerequisite for processing the data. Thus our task was to reformulate the references to provisions of law, with a view to ensuring consistency.[43] Data relating to place of birth, place of residence, and occupation represented a further category of information. Using a gazetteer, we were able to collect data on each of the geographical places featured in the database (e.g., in which county, what kind of settlement, the number of inhabitants).[44] For occupations, we created a code system that enabled us to systemize the more than 1,900 occupations featured in the database. We were then able to categorize them within the occupational structure of interwar Hungarian society.[45]

As already noted in the section on sampling, each year was represented in our analysis by 100 case files. However, the number of case files in each year was not uniform over the period. For this reason, in order to draw conclusions for the whole period, we needed to restore the annual ratio by weighting our analysis.[46]

Preparing the data files for analysis

Having created the initial database, we still needed to complete a number of tasks before we could create the final data files and the variables suitable for the purpose of analysis. In what follows, we seek to present some of these tasks.

---

43   We will not cover in detail here all the errors that arose in connection with the cited provisions of law.
44   In this area too, we encountered many problems. First, we had to cope with the spelling mistakes. Then we found that a surprisingly large number of villages in Hungary have the same name as other villages.
45   We return to this later on when we look at the occupations of defendants.
46   In graphic terms, those files that are overrepresented are taken into account with less weight, while those files that are underrepresented are taken into account with more.

First, we cleansed the data, doing so in several stages. We checked that the encoders had recorded from the data sheets what was necessary based on the contents of the case files. We corrected possible errors and data that was recorded in ways contrary to the instructions. Furthermore, we examined the logical relations between the data, and wherever we found a contradiction, we re-examined the case file.

Since the amount of data was colossal, it could only be processed using algorithms. We required generalized programs that produced the appropriate piece of data for each case. This, in turn, necessitated fully consistent databases. Where there is so much data, the individual handling of cases is ineffective for two reasons. First, it is extremely time-consuming; second, the risk of human error is very high. The algorithms had to be written in such a way that they would function for each type of case and ultimately produce a correct result. The types of cases varied; in one type, there was only one defendant and the trial was held at only one level—that is, there was no appeal. In another type, there was only one defendant, but the trial went to appeal. In cases with multiple defendants, we found a great number of different combinations. Sometimes the number of defendants changed during a trial. At other times, some of the defendants made appeals while others did not.

As pointed out earlier, the initial data file was at the level of the case file. That is to say, a row in the database represented a people's tribunal case file. In the course of the analysis, however, our aim was not only to establish the percentage of trials featuring certain attributes (and correlations between certain of these characteristics) but also to analyze the defendants and witnesses—which required us to create databases relating to both these groups.

In what follows, we present a miniature database showing exactly what we mean. The database for case files had data for defendants at the lower level and at the appeal level on different variables. However, when examining defendants, we wished to draw conclusions for all defendants. In the following 10 case files, there was one accused in five files, two accused in four files, and three accused in one file. For the sake of simplicity, we shall look at only one piece of data: the defendant's gender. The following figure presents the structure of a data file relating to a case file. In this database, we see that the data for the first, second, and third defendants are featured in separate columns. The numeral 1 indicates a male, while the numeral 2 indicates a female. Analysis of this database allows us to make statements concerning the case files. Here, for instance, we can state what we described when defining our example: the number of case files—from among the 10—with one, two, or three defendants.

	Gender of 1st defendant	Gender of 2nd defendant	Gender of 3rd defendant
1. file	1		
2. file	1	1	
3. file	1		
4. file	2		
5. file	1	1	
6. file	2	2	1
7. file	1		
8. file	1		
9. file	1	1	
10. file	2	1	

Figure 3.1 Sample of data file at the level of the case files

Based on the results, we can easily calculate that there were a total of 16 defendants in the 10 case files. However, we cannot state, on the basis of this database, how many of the defendants were male and how many were female.[47] For this we need to establish a database relating to defendants, in which each row represents an accused person rather than a case file. We present this in the following figure. The first column in the table contains the case file number. Since there was just one defendant in case file nos. 1, 3, 4, 7, and 8, these numbers are featured just once. Case files with two defendants (nos. 5, 9, and 10) are shown twice, while the only case file with three defendants (no. 6) is shown three times. This database enables us to examine the gender breakdown of defendants, whereby we find that the 16 defendants consisted of 12 males and four females.

When examining the simple distribution of the defendants' various attributes, it is worth using the database relating to the defendants. Indeed, the use of the same database is unavoidable if we wish to analyze correlations between the various attributes of the defendants. For instance, where we know another variable for the defendants, such as ed-

---

[47] Of course, in such a small database, we could easily have counted them. But in the 500 case files we had 617 defendants placed on 13 variables.

	File no.	Gender of defendant
1. defendant	1	1
2. defendant	2	1
3. defendant	2	1
4. defendant	3	1
5. defendant	4	2
6. defendant	5	1
7. defendant	5	1
8. defendant	6	2
9. defendant	6	2
10. defendant	6	1
11. defendant	7	1
12. defendant	8	1
13. defendant	9	1
14. defendant	9	1
15. defendant	10	2
16. defendant	10	1

Figure 3.2 Sample of data file at the level of defendants

ucational qualifications, we can examine the correlation between the gender and educational level of the defendants. In the course of the analysis, we used two additional databases: a database relating to the witnesses and a database relating to the court hearings.

In many instances, it was very time-consuming to establish the desired variables. For example, let us examine the judgments (sentences) received by the defendants. The decrees and laws regulating the people's tribunals featured 11 different types of sentence: death, maximum-security prison, penitentiary, minimum-security prison, forced labor, internment, the confiscations of assets, a monetary fine, the loss of job or public office, a ban on exercising one's profession, and the suspension of political rights. When examining the case files, we recorded the judgment given to each defendant. We recorded the data, filling out for each accused a sentence data sheet at each level of the trial. For each judgment, we also recorded the basis for the sentence, its type, and whether the defendant was convicted or acquitted. Where the defendant was convicted, we also recorded which of the various types of sentence featured in the judgment and, if required, the length of the sentence. Our task was hampered by the fact that in many instances the defendant had not been indicted for a single offense—that is to say, we were not able to record a single judgment. As already noted, we first had to establish a database relating to the defendant from each case file. Using that database, we then had to establish the variables we wished to employ during the analysis—whether, for instance, a defendant was convicted or acquitted on all counts of the indictment or whether he or she was found guilty on some counts and acquitted on others. For each defendant with at least a partial conviction, we had to establish three variables for each type of sentence: whether the sentence was imposed by a lower court or (where applicable) by the appeal court, or in the final decision. Here the third variable represented the logical combination of the first two—in other words, the final decision was the tribunal's decision at first instance where the trial was completed at the lower level or the appeal court decision where the case went to appeal. For sentences involving time, we also had to consider the duration of the sentence. When establishing these variables, we had to produce a variable row for each of the case file judgments, which were then combined to produce the final variables described above.

Based on our experience in this regard, if we were to undertake such research again, we might ask the encoders to record the data immediately in the final variable. However, while the general use of such an approach in our research would have been practical, it would also have been very dangerous. The approach we employed enabled us to make use of data recorded from the case files in several different ways. If we had recorded only those variables that were intended for analysis, this would have significantly limited the potential for analysis. Obviously, many things become clear after a survey has been completed, but in such pioneer research this option would have been impossible.

Several Notes on the Methodology and the Findings

The data sheets presented clearly show the extent of the data collected on the characteristics of the cases. The results stated in this book are mainly of two types. On the one hand, the ratio or the average of a variable can be stated; that is, we can examine the one-dimensional distributions. On the other hand, various correlations and presumed causal relations among the different characteristics can be examined; that is, we can undertake multi-dimensional analyses.

First, however, we should point out that working "only" with a sample has important effects on the conclusions that can be drawn. Let us look at when one wants to state an average or a percentage. For example, the proportion of female defendants was 18 percent. But this is only an estimated percentage, as we used merely a sample. If we had examined all the files, the figure would be more exact. However, in view of the sampling method described above, this inaccuracy of estimation (statistical error) can be accurately calculated. In the case of an estimated percentage, this means one can determine the range in which the ratio would most likely fall if all the files were to be examined. For instance, as regards female defendants, we can state with a high probability that they represented between 15 and 21 percent of all case files created by the Budapest People's Tribunal.[48]

Relationships between the variables represent another factor to consider. If there is a relationship between two variables, then one can, using statistical means, determine whether the relationship exists once all the files have been analyzed. However, once again it is simply a question of there being a degree of uncertainty surrounding our estimate. Let us look once again at an example: we examine whether there is a relationship between a defendant's membership in the Arrow Cross Party[49] *(Nyilaskeresztes Párt)* or associated organization and whether he or she was born outside Hungary's Trianon borders. In other words, we investigate whether those defendants who came from outside Hungary were more or less likely to have been members of the Arrow Cross than those born in Hungary (within the Trianon borders). We find that 40 percent of defendants from outside Hungary were members of the Arrow Cross Party or an associated organization, while this was true of 41 percent of those born in Hungary. If we had been observing all defendants, then we could state quite simply whether the two percentages were mathematically equal and thus whether there was statistical equivalence. Based on the data, we could state that, although the difference was minimal, those defendants born outside Hungary (outside the Trianon borders) were less likely to have become members of the Arrow Cross Party or an associ-

---

48   This is a confidence interval of 95 percent.
49   The Arrow Cross Party was founded from different right-wing groups on 15 March, 1939 and led by Ferenc Szálasi (1897–1946). A quisling government was installed by the occupying German troops on 15 October, 1944 which was committed to fight on the side of Germans against the Soviets. Szálasi and other leaders of the party were executed as war criminals after the war.

ated organization. However, since we are working with a sample, which means that the notions of mathematical and statistical equality do not coincide, a mathematical discrepancy was not enough for us to claim a statistical difference. In our case, such a claim could only be made if there was a high probability that the difference between the two percentages would be replicated if we observed everyone. We must state that in our example, this is not the case. Indeed, we must conclude that our findings—the figures of 40 percent and 41 percent—are statistically equal even if they are not so mathematically. The reason for this is that the difference between the two values is less than the error variance. Accordingly, we must state that there is no correlation between the two variables under investigation.

The use of an appropriate sampling procedure means, therefore, that we can, based on the sample, draw statistical conclusions relating to the whole. Of course, the values (statistical values) observed based on the sample are merely estimates for the values for the whole population (the parameters). In other words, we cannot be certain that we would receive these values in the event that we observed everyone; our estimates contain a certain degree of error. The size of the error variance depends on the sample/population ratio: an increase in the number of observed elements will lessen the uncertainty of our estimate, thus enhancing its accuracy.

Computerization and the use of the mathematical-statistical apparatus opened up new analytical opportunities. We were able to examine both one-dimensional distributions and statistics as well as relationships and correlations. Multi-level analysis of the data became a possibility, enabling us to undertake one- and multi-dimensional analyses relating both to the case files and to the defendants and witnesses.

The research employed a combination of approaches from several academic fields: historiography, sociology, and statistics. The interdisciplinary nature of the research gave rise to a unique and innovative methodology. The use of representative sampling and a strictly quantitative research paradigm meant that we could draw conclusions based on the observed sample and concerning the complete surviving written material of the Budapest People's Tribunal. Based on the findings of other researchers and experts, we may assume that there were significant differences in the operation of the various people's tribunals in Hungary. This means that our research does not allow us to formulate claims concerning all the people's tribunals that were in operation in the country.

Analysis of the People's Tribunal Cases

Having presented the methods employed in our investigation of the people's tribunals, we shall, in the rest of this volume, make known the results of the analysis. Our aim was to reveal the basic characteristics and features of the operation of the people's tribunals: What trials were held? How long did they last? Who participated in them? What was the composition of the witnesses and how did this affect the trials?

Types of Cases

As we analyzed the data, we soon realized that the trials held by the people's tribunals were far from uniform. This meant that we could not receive an accurate impression of the process by handling the trials together. Consequently, we distinguished five types of trial in the analysis. The classification of trials into types was achieved through a detailed study of the various case files. When classifying the cases, we paid attention both to the recorded data and to the sound files made by the encoders.[50]

The first type included those cases where Jews were the aggrieved parties and where the crime on which the indictment was based took place during World War II (cases related to wartime acts against Jews). This group comprised 43 percent of all cases. The aggrieved parties were identified as Jews by examining religious data in the case file and the nature of the crime committed. Based on the latter piece of information, we could draw conclusions about the religious affinity of the aggrieved

---

50 Meanwhile, our point of departure could only be the alleged crimes; we could not examine whether the contents of the indictments were true.

person even when this was not clearly stated in the written material. We proceeded in the same manner when dealing with the witnesses. Thus in our investigation, we used the category "Jewish" as it was manifested in the operation of the people's tribunals. During the Holocaust, the authorities determined who was and was not Jewish—who was and who was not to be targeted for genocide. The people's tribunals also followed this logic: in attempting to serve justice, they repeated the classification of people as Jews in the process. Since the focus of our research was political justice, we also noted that although a person's religion was not noted on his or her registration at the court, he or she nevertheless came to the court as a "legal party" that had suffered persecution, whereby the category of "persecuted persons" was created. One should note that there was no stigma to self-identifying as a Jew during a trial held by the people's tribunal, as this could assist aggrieved parties and/or witnesses in their struggle to ensure that those who had committed crimes against them, or their relatives or friends, were punished. When making the classification, we also utilized the subjective views of witnesses in the cases, in order to determine whom we should regard as Jewish.

In 26 percent of the case files, the defendants had been members of some kind of far right, arrow cross, armed organizations before 1945 (cases related to membership in the Arrow Cross or an associated organization), and such membership formed the basis of the indictment. The case files did not expressly mention crimes perpetrated against Jews. Even so, we could not exclude the possibility that members of such organizations took part in anti-Jewish acts. Indeed, given the public mood prior to 1945, this is a very likely scenario.

The third type comprises cases where the aggrieved parties were non-Jewish (cases related to acts committed against non-Jews);[51] such cases constitute 12 percent of all cases. Most of these cases concerned matters such as the transfer of factories to German control, pro-German actions by Hungarian soldiers, and criminal acts committed against Soviet soldiers during the war. The fact that four-fifths of such cases concern wartime actions contradicts the claim made by some that the people's tribunals served merely as an instrument of class struggle after the communist takeover (Bernáth 1993).

---

[51] Since anti-Semitism was present throughout society, we may suppose that in many of these cases a link was made with hostility towards Jews, but this was not actually mentioned in the indictments.

Analysis of the People's Tribunal Cases

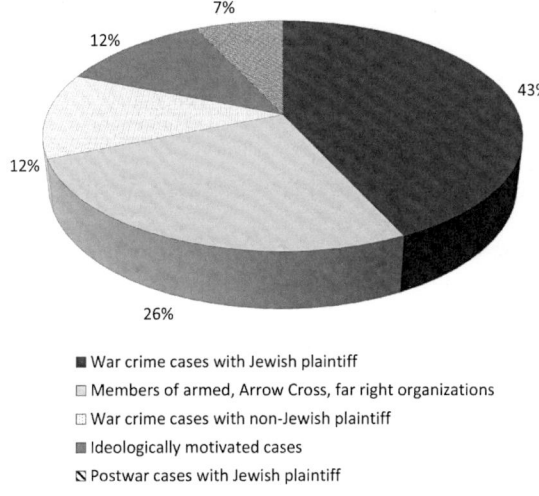

- War crime cases with Jewish plaintiff
- Members of armed, Arrow Cross, far right organizations
- War crime cases with non-Jewish plaintiff
- Ideologically motivated cases
- Postwar cases with Jewish plaintiff

Figure 4.1 Types of trials

Cases included in the fourth and fifth groups relate to acts committed in the aftermath of World War II. This shows the special nature of post–World War II transitional justice in Hungary: the people's tribunals not only examined wartime crimes but also launched a war against enemies of the nascent totalitarian regime, having reinterpreted the war as an unfinished process and based in particular on the provisions of Act VII of 1946. The fourth group of cases comprises what are known as the ideological trials, which began after the entry into force of Act VII of 1946 and whose purpose was to silence the political opposition.[52] Such trials account for 12 percent of the total. Cases involving crimes committed after the war against Jewish aggrieved parties (cases related to acts committed against Jews in the postwar period) comprise 7 percent of all cases. Some of these latter cases might also be classified as ideological trials.

Distribution of the types of cases over time

The distribution of the different types of trial varied over time. In 1945—the first year of the operation of the people's tribunals—cases related to wartime acts against Jews predominated. Whereas 43 percent of

---

52 Some of the cases were related to crimes in the postwar period and were ideological in nature but also related to crimes against Jews. These were now placed in the category of cases related to crimes against Jews in the postwar period.

47

all cases surveyed were of this type, the figure for cases launched in 1945 was 55 percent. In 1946, greater emphasis was given to cases related to acts committed against non-Jews: whereas 12 percent of all cases surveyed were of this type, the figure for cases launched in 1946 was 18 percent. In 1947, it seems that the emphasis switched to membership in the Arrow Cross and associated organizations: whereas 26 percent of all surveyed cases were of this type, the figure for cases launched in 1947 was 37 percent. While the ideological trials were launched soon after the adoption of Act VII of 1946, it was not until 1948—the year of the communist takeover—that such trials were seen in large numbers. Indeed, we found that ideological trials accounted for 18 percent of trials

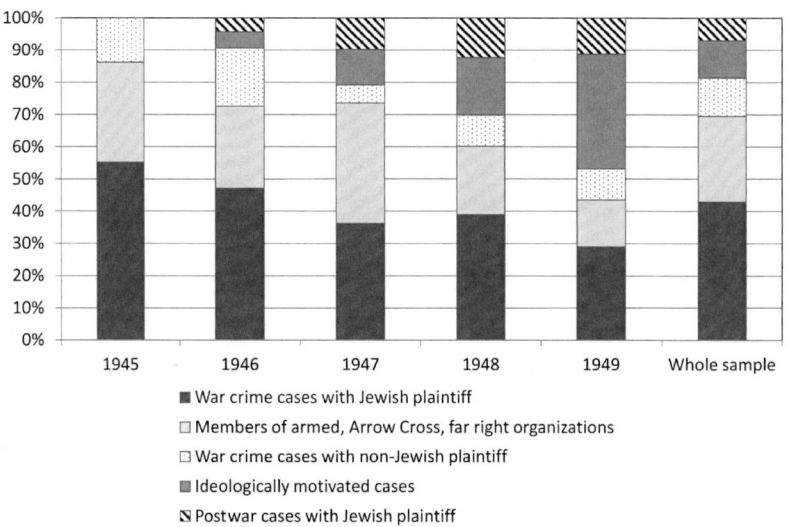

Figure 4.2 Types of trials over time

launched in 1948 (as opposed to 12 percent of the whole sample). Also characteristic in 1948 were trials related to acts committed against Jews in the postwar period. It is interesting to observe that in 1949—when the communist dictatorship was already established—the percentage of ideological trials increased further: 35 percent of cases launched in that year were of this type. On the other hand, in the same year, cases related to acts committed against Jews in the postwar period were no more typical than average. This seems to indicate that the trial and punishment of those accused of verbal anti-Semitism had indeed been a byproduct of the struggle against the "enemies of democracy." With the completion of this struggle and the consolidation of communist dictatorship, such trials were no longer deemed necessary.

Characteristics of the Case Files

The surveyed case files contained, on average, 86 pages. The shortest had 14 pages, while the longest had 404 pages. We found that the average length of the case files varied depending on the type of case. The longest case files—100–110 pages on average—were for cases related to wartime acts committed against Jews or non-Jews. Case files in cases related to membership in the Arrow Cross or an associated organization contained 65 pages on average. Case files in cases related to postwar acts were shorter: on average, case files in the ideological trials contained 60 pages, while those in cases related to acts committed against Jews in the postwar period contained around 70 pages.

When processing the case files, we also recorded their content. An indictment (charges) and a judgment (sentence) were found in almost all the case files. Meanwhile, a report was found in 80 percent of the case files, a request or petition in almost three-quarters, a denunciation in almost a quarter, and a notification report in 5 percent.

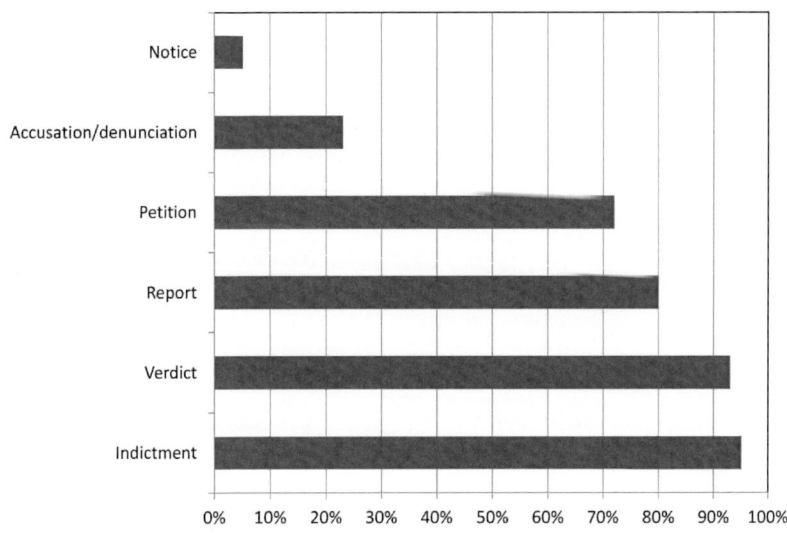

Figure 4.3 Content of the case files

In terms of the content of case files, we found three differences between the various types of cases. Case files in cases related to wartime acts against Jews were more likely than average to contain a denunciation: the figure for such cases was 37 percent, compared with 23 percent for the whole sample. Such case files were also more likely than average to contain reports (86 percent) and requests/petitions (83 percent). Only 9 percent of case files for cases related to membership in the Arrow Cross or an associated organization contained a denunciation, which is significantly below the average. Such case files were also less likely than average to contain reports (71 percent) or requests/petitions (59 percent). Case files for ideological trials were more likely than average to contain reports (80 percent) but less likely than average to contain a denunciation (17 percent). In such case files, requests/petitions were less likely to be present (53 percent) than on average in the whole sample. The case files for cases related to acts committed against Jews or non-Jews in the postwar period were of average content in all of the respects indicated above.

Analysis of the Various Actors in the People's Tribunals

Defendants

In the 500 cases surveyed, 617 defendants were put on trial. In 90 percent of the case files, there is only one defendant. In the course of our analysis, we were not in a position to say whether the charges in a case were true or false. Thus, we could not claim to know whether there was only one defendant because he or she was the sole perpetrator or because he or she was the only one to be apprehended among several perpetrators. We found that the average number of defendants did not vary according to the type of case. On the other hand, we did find discrepancies when we distinguished between single-defendant and multiple-defendant cases. The difference was noticeable in cases related to wartime acts, while the distribution was average for cases related to postwar acts. Cases related to acts committed against Jews or acts committed against non-Jews were more likely than average to have multiple defendants, while cases related to membership in the Arrow Cross or an associated organization were less likely to have multiple defendants: indeed, only 4 percent of such cases featured multiple defendants.

Gender ratios

In general, our analysis of post-World War II transitional justice focused on political history rather than social history. An important development was the emergence of female perpetrators—in quite a high ratio. At the people's tribunals, 18 percent of defendants were women. However, in cases related to membership in the Arrow Cross or an associated organization, only 9 percent of defendants were women. In cases related to acts committed against Jews, the male-female ratio did not differ from the ratio for the sample as a whole. We did find, however, a difference in terms of the types of crime committed, which seems to confirm social gender stereotypes. Physical violence was the only type of crime typically committed by men rather than by women (it was mentioned in 48 percent of indictments against men, compared with 23 percent of indictments against women). Denunciations were more typical in cases involving women than in cases involving men (55 percent of cases involving women, compared with 27 percent of cases involving men). Women were also overrepresented in crimes committed for financial gain (42 percent of cases involving women, compared with 35 percent of cases involving men) (cf. Karsai 2004, 70).

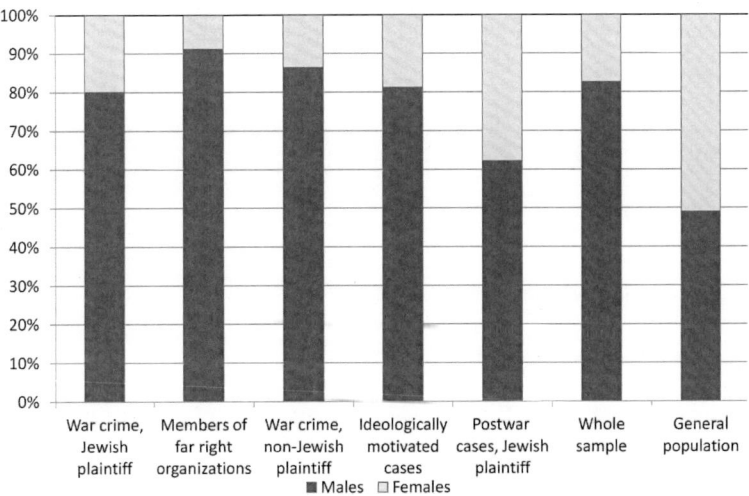

Figure 4.4 Gender ratios of defendants by trial types and in the whole sample, and gender ratio of the general population[53]

---

53 In the figure, we indicate the types of cases as follows: 1. cases related to wartime acts against Jews; 2. cases related to membership in the Arrow Cross or an associated organization; 3. cases related to acts committed against non-Jews; 4. the ideological trials; 5. cases related to acts committed against Jews in the postwar period. These categories are used henceforth.

The data show that in cases related to postwar acts committed against Jews, the proportion of women was higher than average (38 percent). We thought this might have been due to the fact that in all these cases the accusation concerned—in part—verbal anti-Semitism, and women were often among those who reacted to the Communist Party's campaign against black marketeers by spouting anti-Jewish abuse in public spaces and at markets (Palasik 2000). On the other hand, in cases related to wartime acts against Jews, we find that such behavior was not significantly more characteristic of women. The reason for the gender difference in the postwar figures appears to have been the changing milieu: Act VII of 1946 altered the rules governing hate speech, in effect feminizing it. The wartime acts committed against Jews tended to have been robbery and murder—two types of crime not typically carried out by women. By contrast, after the war, verbal abuse of Jews was generally the crime that led women to be put on trial. Later on in the study, we will examine in more detail the gendered aspects of the operation of the people's tribunals.

Age distribution

The average age of defendants was 38 years. Regarding the demographic profile, it should be noted that we compared the percentages found in our investigation with the country's general population at the time—that is, with the census data. Regarding defendants, we found that middle-aged persons (those born between 1896 and 1915) were overrepresented. Whereas this age group represented 36 percent of the country's general population based on the census data for 1930,[54] 54 percent of defendants in trials held by the people's tribunals were in this age group. The overrepresentation of this age group among defendants was mirrored in the underrepresentation of the oldest age group (those born before 1896). Meanwhile, the percentage for the youngest group—those aged less than 30 years in 1945—was equal to that for the whole population.

We identified, therefore, an evident overrepresentation of middle-aged persons among defendants. Still, let us first examine the differences between defendants in the various types of trial. In cases related to acts committed against Jews in the postwar period, we found relatively few

---

54   We compared our data, whenever possible, with the 1930 census data. This was because the country's borders at the time of the census corresponded with those of the postwar era. The census was carried out after the Trianon peace treaty but before the re-annexation of territory by Hungary.

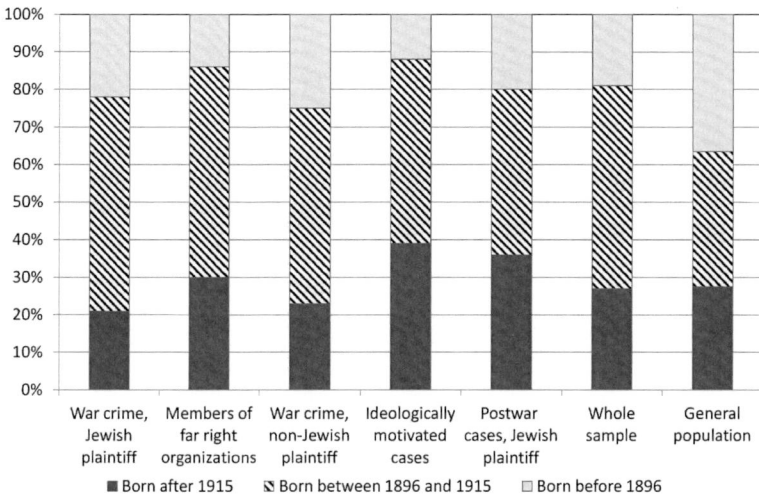

Figure 4.5 Age distribution of defendants by trial types and in the whole sample, and age distribution of the general population

young defendants. The 21 percent share for this age group was somewhat less than its percentage of the whole sample (26 percent). For the other two types of wartime cases, the age distribution of defendants did not differ significantly from that for the whole sample. However, we found a significant difference in cases related to postwar acts: here the proportion of young people was greater than in the whole sample.

Place of birth

The trials investigated in our research were those held by the Budapest People's Tribunal.[55] In view of this fact, the overrepresentation of people born in rural areas was particularly striking. Whereas 48 percent of the general population had been born in a rural area, we found that the corresponding figure among defendants was 60 percent. We did not observe large differences in the share of those born in Budapest and in other major cities. The real difference emerged with respect to those born in small towns: the figure was 23 percent for the general population but only 12 percent among defendants.

---

55 The territorial jurisdiction of the Budapest People's Tribunal covered the area falling under the Budapest Criminal Court and the Pest County Court. Although beginning in 1947 the cases of other people's tribunals (those terminated because of an insufficient number of cases) were redirected to the Budapest People's Tribunal, most of the surveyed cases were from the Budapest area or from Pest County.

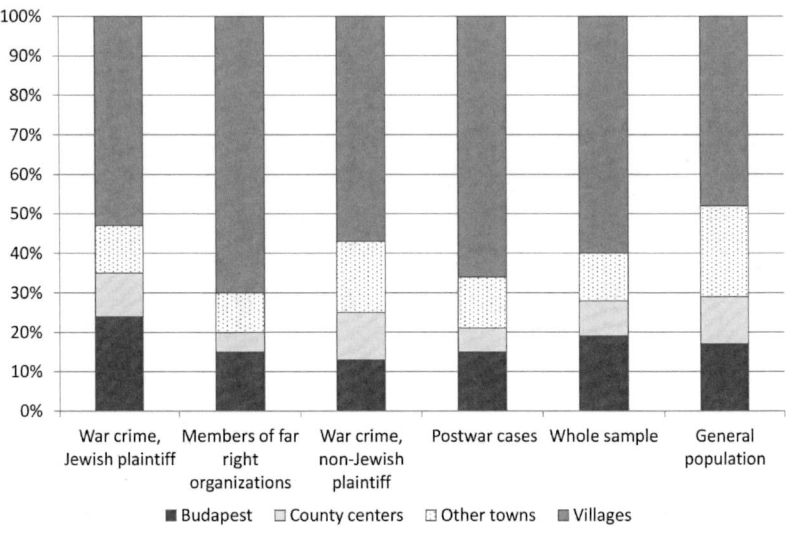

Figure 4.6 Birthplace distribution of defendants by trial types and in the whole sample, and birthplace distribution of the general population[56]

When comparing the various types of cases, we see that in cases related to wartime acts against Jews, defendants were more likely to have been born in Budapest. Here the share of those born in a rural area was less than the average (53 percent), but it still exceeded by a significant margin the percentage for the population as a whole. In cases related to membership in the Arrow Cross or an associated organization, we found that a high percentage of defendants came from rural areas. Indeed, in such cases, as many as 70 percent of defendants came from such areas. Concerning the defendants in cases related to acts committed against non-Jews and to postwar crimes, the ratios we found were typical of the whole sample.

We also examined the birthplace of defendants from an additional angle, namely whether it was inside or outside Hungary's Trianon borders. We found that 18 percent of defendants had been born outside the Trianon borders, whereas according to the 1930 population census data, only 7 percent of the general population had been born outside Hungary at that time.[57] Among such defendants, we found an overrepresen-

---

56 In view of the small sample size, we were forced to merge types 4 and 5. The birthplace distribution of defendants in the two types of cases did not differ significantly.
57 The percentage of people born outside Hungary was the same in the 1949 census.

tation of people aged over 50 and an overrepresentation of the better educated and those with relatively high social status. We found there were two types of cases that typically had an overrepresentation of defendants born outside Hungary (outside Hungary's Trianon borders): cases related to membership in the Arrow Cross or an associated organization and cases related to acts committed against non-Jews.

Level of education

Defendants were typically better educated than the average for the general population.[58] While 11 percent of the general population had not attended elementary school and a further 70 percent had not completed elementary school, the corresponding figures for defendants were 8 percent and 47 percent. The percentage of defendants with an eighth-grade education roughly coincided with the percentage for the general population. On the other hand, we found that the share of defendants with high school diplomas or university degrees was far higher than the corresponding figure for the general population. Whereas only 5 percent of the general population had a high school diploma and only 1 percent a university degree, the same ratios among defendants were 16 percent and 11 percent.

A comparison of the various types of trials revealed further interesting differences in the various ratios. For instance, defendants in cases related to wartime acts against Jews did not exhibit, in all respects, the strong educational profile observed for defendants in general. While they too were typically well educated, there was a significant difference: among such defendants, people with an eighth-grade education were overrepresented (20 percent) in comparison with defendants in other types of cases. Similarly, among defendants in cases related to membership in the Arrow Cross or an associated organization, those with less than eight grades of education were overrepresented

---

58 Here too we used the 1930 census data—those relating to people aged 20 or over. Usage of the data was hindered by the fact that the Hungarian Central Statistical Office (HCSO) uses the postwar educational categories when giving prewar educational qualifications. We corresponded our data to the census data as follows: did not even complete the first year of elementary school = no educational qualifications, literate; less than eight grades of elementary school (this does not feature directly in the HCSO data, but we deduced it from other data) = four grades of elementary, six grades of elementary; eight grades of elementary = four grades of high school, four grades of middle school (*polgári iskola*); high school diploma = high school diploma, teachers' training college, vocational school diploma; university or college degree = military academy, college, university. In our analysis, we also employed the terminology used by the HCSO.

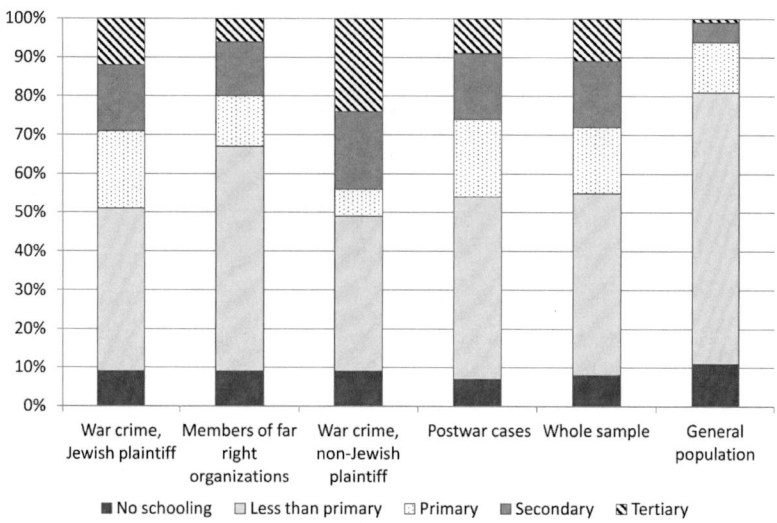

Figure 4.7 Educational level of defendants by trial types and in the whole sample, and educational level of the general population[59]

in relation to the sample as a whole. Indeed, whereas 47 percent of all defendants were in this category, the corresponding figure for defendants in such cases was 58 percent. The educational level of defendants in cases related to acts committed against non-Jews was exceptionally high, even in relation to defendants in other cases. Indeed, in such cases, almost a quarter of defendants had a university degree, whereas this was true of 12 percent of all defendants and just 1 percent of the general population. The defendants' level of education in cases related to postwar acts resembled the average level of education for the whole sample.

Social status

In the absence of other data and indicators, the social status of defendants was classified by occupation. When processing the case files, the encoders recorded the occupations of defendants, noting more than 1,900 different occupations. We then grouped the various occupations in a hierarchy representing interwar society. The top level of the hierarchy was the occupational sector, while the second level consisted of the various subsectors and the lowest level consisted of the occupations

---

59   The small number of cases meant we had to merge types 4 and 5.

themselves. We also attempted to distinguish between the self-employed, managers, and employees, as in our view such differences greatly influenced defendants' position in society. At the sectoral level, we developed the following categories: primary production, mining and metallurgy, industry, trade and commerce, banking and insurance, public service and freelance, armed forces and police, domestic staff, unemployed, and old-age and disability pensioners. A code system enabled us to place the various occupations on the various levels of the social hierarchy with relative certainty. In doing so, we once again took the structure of interwar society into consideration. For instance, we regarded industrial and agricultural workers, day laborers, and domestic maids as working class, self-employed artisans, retailers, and non-commissioned officers as lower middle class, and public servants (public officials) and company managers as middle class. Finally, we considered company owners, senior managers, and senior officers to have been a part of the social elite. When developing these social groups or classes, we inevitably had to create a class of "dependents," in which we placed students, homemakers, and those self-identifying as dependents. This latter group was very heterogeneous; those placed in it had diverse social status, and so the group did not constitute a hierarchical level.[60]

Based on the above categories, 34 percent of defendants were working class, one-fifth were lower middle class, 29 percent were middle class, and 5 percent belonged to the social elite. Dependents made up just over 10 percent of defendants. The figures for the various types of cases differed significantly. In cases related to wartime acts against Jews, lower-middle-class defendants were overrepresented (26 percent). The working class was overrepresented among defendants accused of membership in the Arrow Cross or an associated organization: whereas the working-class share for the whole sample was 34 percent, it was almost half (47 percent) for such defendants. Defendants of high social status were overrepresented in cases related to acts committed against non-Jews. In such cases, 44 percent of defendants were middle class (compared with 29 percent of the whole sample), and 9 percent belonged to the social elite (compared with 5 percent of the whole sample). In the ideological trials, we found a high percentage of dependents among defendants, which is not surprising given that, as already noted, female

---

60   The encoding of witnesses' occupations and the defining of their social status were achieved in the same way.

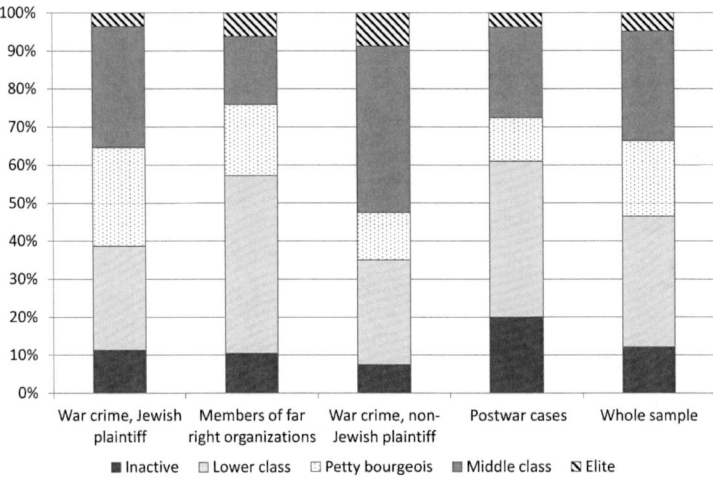

Figure 4.8 Social status of defendants by trial types and in the whole sample, and social status of the general population[61]

perpetrators were overrepresented in such trials. In terms of the age distribution, we found an overrepresentation of working-class people and dependents among defendants in the youngest age group. The distribution was average among middle-aged defendants, but there was an overrepresentation of people belonging to the social elite among defendants in the oldest age group.

Membership in the Arrow Cross

We based our definition of Arrow Cross membership on Act VIII of 1945, which named those organizations whose members and officials were to forfeit their electoral rights.[62] Within this definition, we established two sub-definitions. The first included membership in the Volksbund,[63] while the second ignored such membership. Among Hungary's ethnic German population, membership in the Volksbund had been almost automatic; in other words, it did not necessarily reflect a

---

61 The small number of cases meant that we had to merge types 4 and 5.
62 In addition to the organizations mentioned in the legislation, we also included the Death Head Legion (*Halálfejes Légió*), the Hungarist Legion (*Hungarista Légió*), the Hungarist Movement (*Hungarista Mozgalom*), the Hungaria Fraternity, and the National Front (*Nemzeti Front*).
63 Volksbund (*Volksbund der Deutschen in Ungarn*) was the organization of the German minority founded in 1938. The Volksbund was founded as a National Socialist organization, however many ethnic Germans considered it as an advocacy organization. After WWII leaders of the Volksbund were persecuted and their membership list was used for forced resettlement of ethnic Germans in Hungary.

conscious decision or an ideological commitment. Overall, 41 percent of defendants had been members of the Arrow Cross Party *(Nyilaskeresztes Párt)* or an associated organization. When we included membership in the Volksbund, this figure increased to 48 percent.

Whichever categorization we used, we found that defendants who were once Arrow Cross members were almost always being tried in cases related to wartime acts. In cases related to postwar acts, we identified only eight defendants who had definitely been members of the Arrow Cross Party or an associated organization. Meanwhile, 48 percent of defendants in the first three types of cases had been members of the Arrow Cross Party or an associated organization. The figure increased to 57 percent when we included membership in the Volksbund.

We recorded membership in the Arrow Cross in two ways. First, there was a question relating to such membership on the form filled out about defendants, and so we recorded whether Arrow Cross membership was mentioned there. Second, we also noted whether, during the trial, any information had arisen concerning Arrow Cross membership. The Arrow Cross membership ratio was lower among defendants in cases related to postwar acts, because data relating to such membership was often missing in such cases. This, in turn, reflects the fact that in such cases the data was less likely to be recorded on the official forms and that in the course of such cases, information concerning Arrow Cross membership was less likely to emerge. For all these reasons, in the following, we focus our analysis on the first three types of cases.

The figures clearly show that the two-fold categorization gave rise to a discrepancy only with regard to the second type of case: 57 percent of defendants in such cases had been members of the Arrow Cross or an associated organization, but the figure increased by 25 percentage points if we included membership in the Volksbund. This means that membership in the Volksbund was rarely related to other types of crime. The question arises, however, as to the identity of those making up the remaining 20 percent in the second type of case. We knew that these defendants had not been members of the organizations identified in Act VIII of 1945, and so we concluded that they had been members of the Wehrmacht, the SS or the SS "Hunyadi" Division.[64]

---

64 Under Section 13(4) of the PMDPJ, a war criminal was a person "who, even though he was a Hungarian citizen, joined the German army or the security service (SS, Gestapo, etc.)."

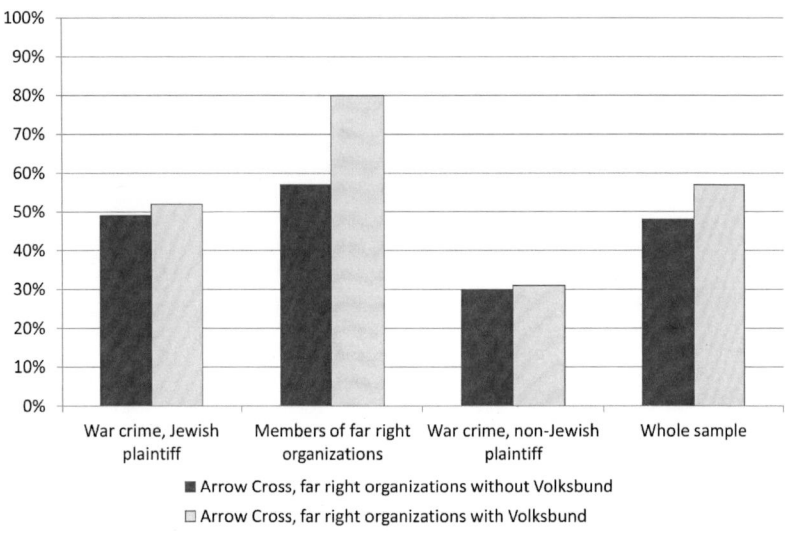

Figure 4.9 Defendants by membership of Arrow Cross in the whole sample and by trial types

The incidence of Arrow Cross membership was average among defendants in cases related to acts committed against Jews. In cases related to acts against non-Jews, around one-third of defendants had been members of the Arrow Cross Party or an associated organization. It is interesting to examine the demographics of former Arrow Cross members who were defendants in trials held by the people's tribunals. Aside from a higher incidence of membership among the male defendants, we found no other correlation with a demographic variable. In other words, the demographics of defendants who had been members of the Arrow Cross Party or an associated organization did not differ from the demographics of defendants who had not been members of such bodies.

Witnesses

In the 500 cases surveyed, 3,668 witnesses were heard. Thus on average, there were seven witnesses in each case. In this regard, we found significant differences between the various types of cases. The number of witnesses was highest in cases related to wartime acts against Jews: in such cases there were on average 10 witnesses. Two-thirds of such cases featured more than five witnesses, and in 34 percent there were more than 10 witnesses. The average number of witnesses in cases related to acts

Analysis of the People's Tribunal Cases

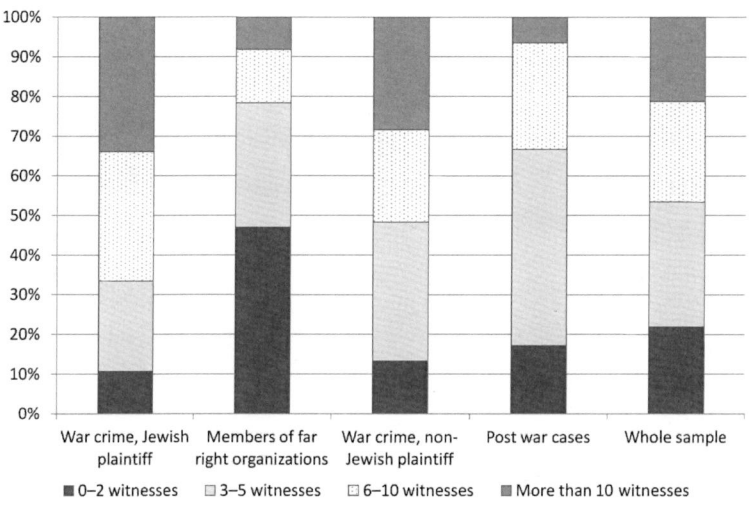

Figure 4.10 Number of witnesses in the whole sample and by trial types

committed against non-Jews was also high (nine witnesses), while the distribution of such cases by category was average, with three to five witnesses in 35 percent of such cases and more than 10 witnesses in 28 percent of such cases. In cases related to membership in the Arrow Cross or an associated organization, only four witnesses were heard on average. In almost half of such cases, there were two or fewer witnesses. It seems that in such cases the prosecution's evidence was based, at least in part, on the membership records of the organizations themselves. In cases related to postwar acts, the average number of witnesses was around five, while three to five witnesses were heard in almost half of such cases.

Gender ratios

Overall, 26 percent of witnesses were women. However, the distribution was not uniform among the various types of cases. In cases related to wartime acts against Jews, the female proportion of witnesses is somewhat higher (30 percent), while it is significantly lower in cases related to other wartime acts. Women account for 22 percent of witnesses in cases related to membership in the Arrow Cross or an associated organization and 16 percent of witnesses in cases related to acts committed against non-Jews. In cases related to postwar acts, the gender ratio does not differ from the ratio for the whole sample.

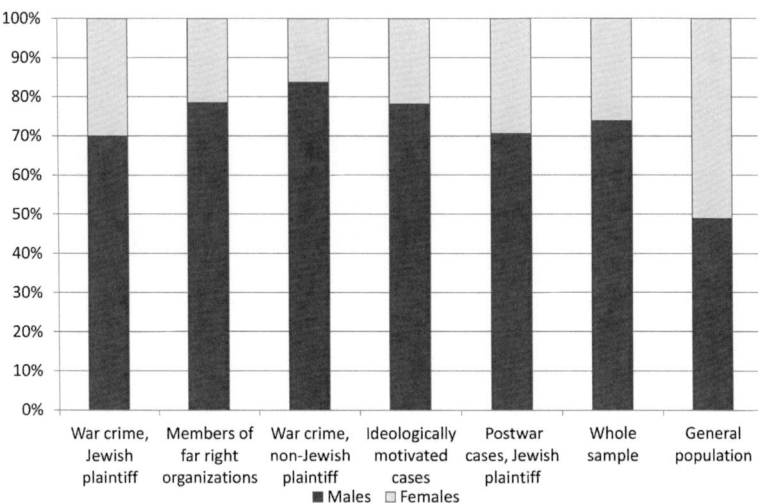

Figure 4.11 Gender ratios of witnesses by trial types and in the whole sample, and gender ratio of the general population

Age distribution

The average age of the witnesses was 41 years. Middle-aged people (i.e., those born between 1896 and 1915) were overrepresented among witnesses in comparison with their share of the general population. People in this age group made up 54 percent of witnesses in the cases surveyed but only 36 percent of the general population.

We found differences between the various types of cases. In cases related to wartime acts against Jews, the proportion of witnesses in the youngest age group (17 percent) was less than the corresponding figure for the sample as a whole. The age distribution of witnesses in cases related to membership in the Arrow Cross or an associated organization was average. In cases related to acts committed against non-Jews, young people were overrepresented among the witnesses: their share was 25 percent, compared with 21 percent for the sample as a whole. In such cases, the share of middle-aged witnesses (50 percent) was slightly less than their share of the whole sample. The biggest difference, however, was observed in cases related to postwar acts. In such cases, there was an overrepresentation of young witnesses (around 35 percent); this figure was significantly higher than the share of young people in the whole sample (28 percent). In the ideological trials, we found, furthermore, an

Analysis of the People's Tribunal Cases

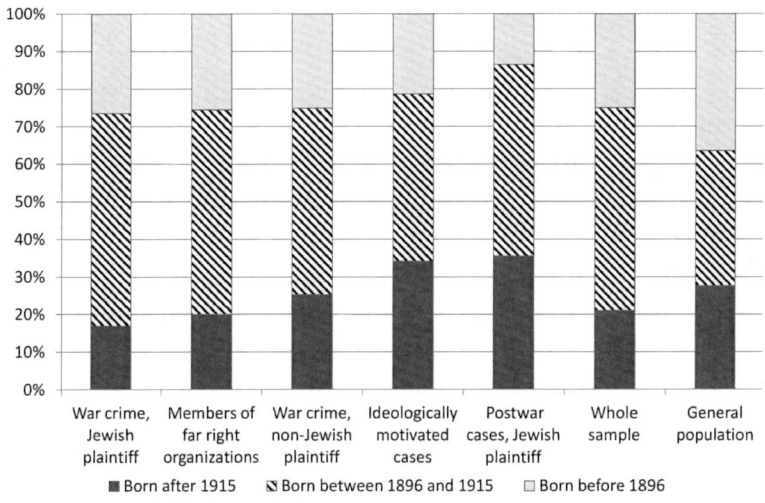

Figure 4.12 Age distribution of witnesses by trial types and in the whole sample, and age distribution of the general population

underrepresentation of the two other age groups. In such cases, 45 percent of witnesses were middle-aged, compared with 54 percent of the whole sample, while people in the oldest age group accounted for 21 percent of witnesses, compared with 25 percent of the whole sample. In cases related to acts committed against Jews in the postwar period, the share of middle-aged witnesses was average, while people in the oldest age group were underrepresented (14 percent) in comparison with their share of the whole sample.

Place of birth

Our analysis showed that the percentage of witnesses born in Budapest was significantly higher than the corresponding percentage for the general population. This was not surprising, given that we were examining trials held by the Budapest People's Tribunal and that Jewish witnesses were often heard in such cases. After the Holocaust, the share of the Jewish population born in Budapest was very high. Whereas one in four of the witnesses had been born in Budapest, this was true for only 17 percent of the general population. The share of witnesses born in rural areas roughly coincided with the corresponding figure for the general population, but people born in urban areas outside Budapest were un-

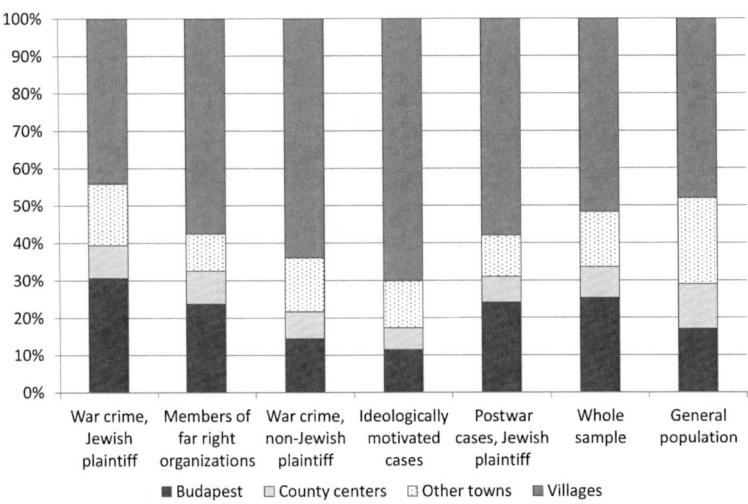

Figure 4.13 Birthplace distribution of witnesses by trial types and in the whole sample, and birthplace distribution of the general population

derrepresented among witnesses. In the cases surveyed, 15 percent of witnesses came from such urban areas, whereas the corresponding figure for the general population was 23 percent.

Striking differences between witnesses in the various types of cases were observed. In cases related to wartime acts against Jews, we found an overrepresentation among witnesses of people born in Budapest and an underrepresentation of people born in rural areas. In such cases, 31 percent of witnesses had been born in Budapest and 44 percent in rural areas, whereas the corresponding figures for the whole sample were 25 percent and 52 percent. In the other types of cases, among witnesses we found an overrepresentation of people born in rural areas. This also applied in cases related to acts committed against non-Jews and in the ideological postwar trials. In the former, 64 percent of witnesses came from rural areas, while in the latter 70 percent did so. In these two types of cases, the percentages of witnesses born in Budapest were correspondingly low (14 percent and 11 percent).

Social status

Since the educational qualifications of witnesses were unknown, we were limited to using the occupational indicator to characterize their social position. We found that 16 percent of witnesses were dependents,

Analysis of the People's Tribunal Cases

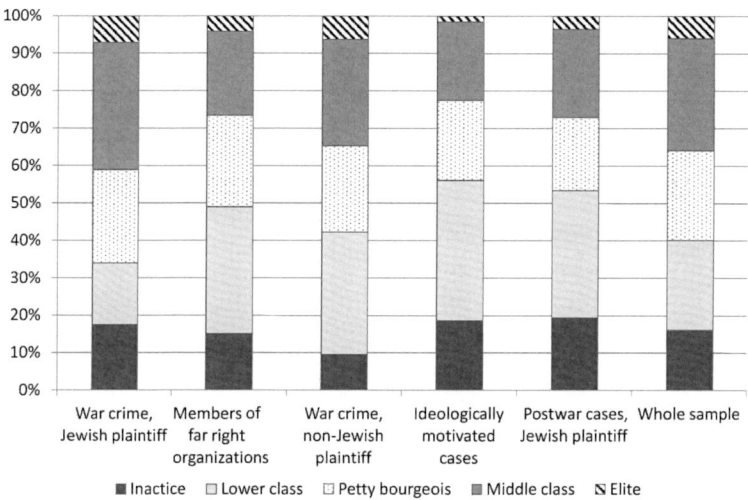

Figure 4.14 Social status of witnesses by trial types and in the whole sample, and social status of the general population

24 percent were working class, 24 percent were lower middle class, 30 percent were middle class, and 6 percent belonged to the social elite. Among witnesses in cases related to wartime acts against Jews, we found an overrepresentation of dependents and an overrepresentation of people belonging to the social elite, but the deviation from the average was not particularly great. In both instances, there were obvious reasons for the discrepancy. As already noted, in such cases a relatively high proportion of witnesses were Jews, whose social status, as a group, tended to be higher than average. Furthermore, we have already seen that women were often witnesses in these cases, as a consequence of which there was a relatively high share of dependents. In all other types of cases, working-class people were overrepresented among witnesses.

Summary of the Demographics of Defendants and Witnesses in the Various Types of Cases

The female ratio was slightly higher among the witnesses (26 percent) than among the defendants (18 percent). The greatest differences in the gender distributions for defendants and witnesses were observed in cases related to wartime acts against Jews and in cases related to membership in the Arrow Cross or an associated organization. In the former, women

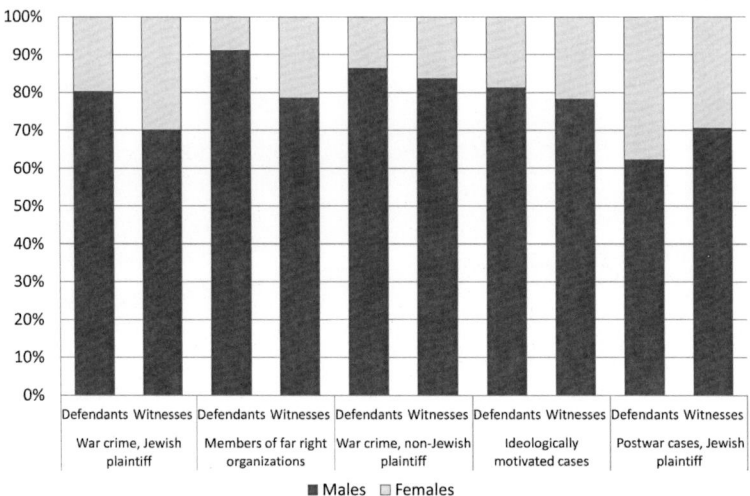

Figure 4.15 Comparison of gender ratios of defendants and witnesses by trial types and witnesses

made up one-fifth of defendants but 30 percent of witnesses. In the latter, women made up slightly less than one-tenth of defendants but more than one-fifth of witnesses.

Among both defendants and witnesses, we found significant overrepresentations of middle-aged people (i.e., people born between 1896 and 1915). This age group accounted for 54 percent of the total in both instances. Differences were observed, however, in the respective percentages of the other two age groups. In the case of defendants, we found an overrepresentation of the oldest age group, while the percentage of young people corresponded with the figure for the general population. Meanwhile, among witnesses, both young people and the oldest age group were underrepresented in comparison with the general population census data. In cases related to wartime acts committed against Jews and committed against non-Jews, we observed similar age distributions for both defendants and witnesses.[65] In cases related to membership in the Arrow Cross or an associated organization, young people made up 30 percent of defendants but only 20 percent of wit-

---

65 It should be underscored—and this is true for all such findings—that this is the case despite the fact that otherwise the age distributions for the defendants and witnesses differ from each other. However, this is not our concern here; rather, our aim is to compare the various demographic variables of the defendants and witnesses.

nesses. In such cases, the oldest age group (i.e., people born before 1896) made up 14 percent of defendants but 26 percent of witnesses. In the ideological trials, we found that those in the oldest age group accounted for a smaller percentage of defendants (12 percent) and a larger percentage of witnesses (21 percent). In cases related to wartime acts against Jews, the overrepresentation of middle-aged people is particularly notable among witnesses (51 percent) and weaker among defendants (44 percent). In such cases, the reverse situation can be observed among the oldest age group, with older people accounting for only 13 percent of witnesses but 20 percent of defendants.

Among defendants, we found a clear overrepresentation of people from rural areas, whereas among witnesses the rural share was roughly the same as for the general population. The reason for this is evidently that people from rural areas were relatively unlikely to be witnesses in cases related to wartime acts against Jews, while 57 percent of all witnesses (i.e., 2,000 of 3,600 witnesses) gave evidence in cases of this type. If we exclude such cases, we find once again a higher ratio of people from rural areas among the witnesses than among the general population. Comparing the places of birth of defendants and witnesses in the various types of cases, we find significant differences. For instance, in cases related to wartime acts against Jews, the defendants were far more

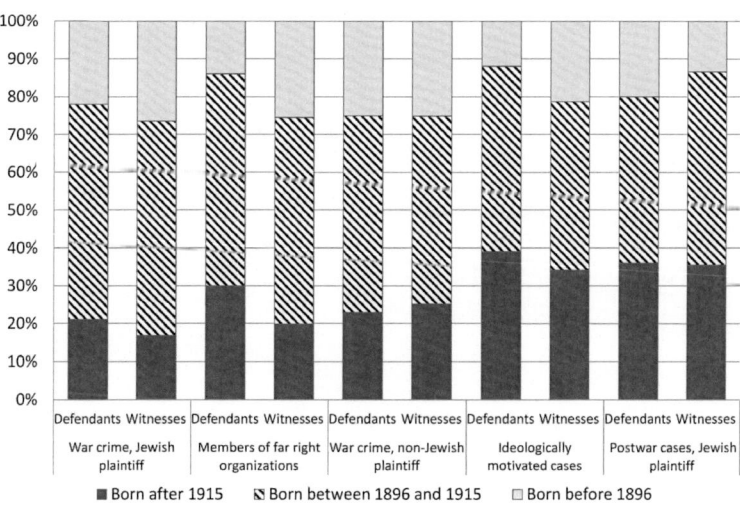

Figure 4.16 Comparison of age distributions of defendants and witnesses by trial types

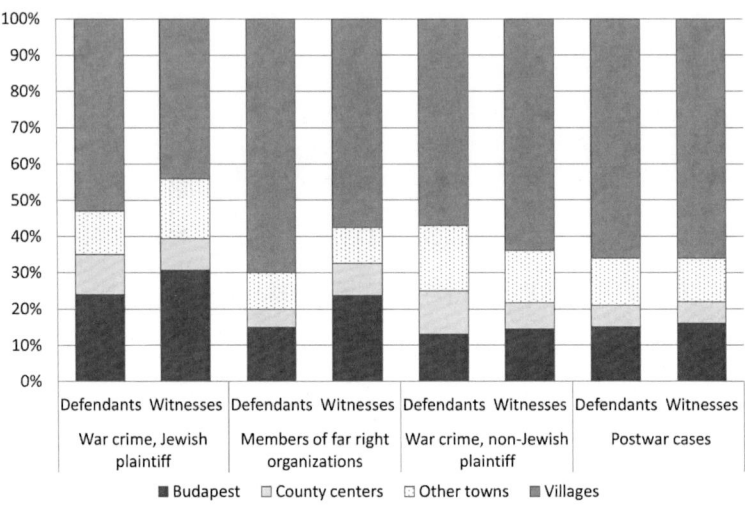

Figure 4.17 Comparison of birthplaces of defendants and witnesses by trial types

likely to come from rural areas, while the witnesses were more likely to come from Budapest. In cases related to membership in the Arrow Cross or an associated organization, the share of defendants from rural areas was particularly high (70 percent), while people from Budapest were overrepresented among witnesses (24 percent). In terms of birthplace, defendants and witnesses showed the greatest similarity in cases related to acts committed against non-Jews. Examining cases related to postwar acts,[66] we found no difference in terms of the birthplace distribution between defendants and witnesses. However, we also noted that the proportion of people from rural areas was higher (70 percent) and the proportion of people from Budapest lower (11 percent) among witnesses in the ideological trials than among witnesses in cases related to acts committed against Jews in the postwar period. Among the latter, the respective figures were 58 percent and 24 percent.

For reasons we have already outlined, in cases related to wartime acts against Jews, we found overrepresentations among witnesses of people of higher social status and of dependants. Furthermore, in cases related to membership in the Arrow Cross and in cases related to acts committed against non-Jews, we found an overrepresentation of working-class witnesses, but in both types of cases this was fully unrelated to

---

66 As far as defendants are concerned, the number of cases clearly makes this necessary.

Analysis of the People's Tribunal Cases

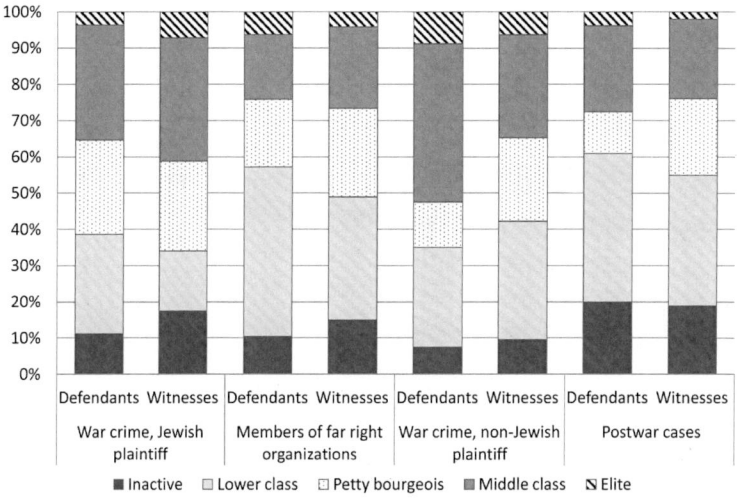

Figure 4.18 Comparison of social status of defendants and witnesses by trial types

the social makeup of defendants. Indeed, in the first group of cases, whereas 47 percent of defendants were working class, this was true of only 34 percent of witnesses. Here, witnesses were more likely to be dependents, lower middle class or middle class. In cases related to acts committed against non-Jews, witnesses were more likely to be working class than were defendants: 33 percent of witnesses in such cases were working class, compared with 28 percent of defendants. In addition, in these cases, we observed stark disparities in the lower-middle-class and middle-class ratios. Thus, whereas only 13 percent of defendants were lower middle class, we found that this was true of 23 percent of witnesses. And whereas 44 percent of defendants were middle class, this was true of only 28 percent of witnesses.

Lawyers

For 23 percent of the defendants, we found no information concerning the lawyers. In the proceedings of the remaining 478 defendants, there were a total of 671 lawyers. Forty-one percent of these lawyers were appointed public defenders, while 59 percent were paid lawyers. These ratios varied, depending on the type of case. The proportion of paid lawyers was slightly higher in cases related to wartime acts against Jews (65 percent) and significantly higher in cases related to acts committed

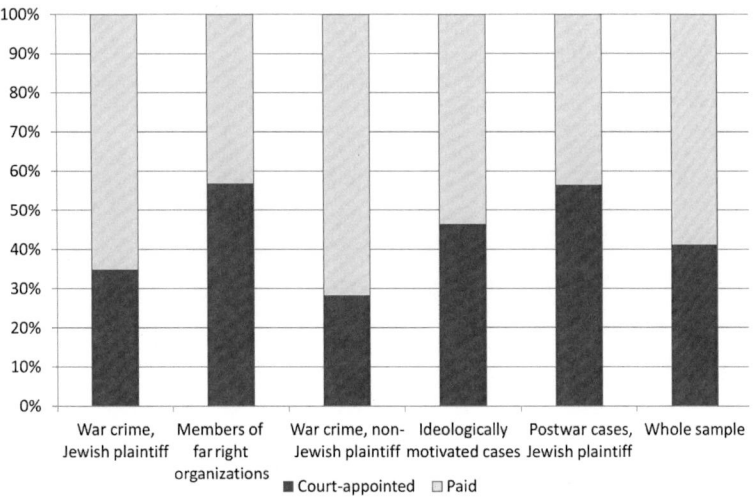

Figure 4.19 Appointed public defenders and paid lawyers by trial types

against non-Jews (72 percent). In cases related to Arrow Cross membership, the proportion of paid lawyers was less than the average for the whole sample (43 percent). In cases related to postwar acts, the proportion of paid lawyers was higher in the ideological trials (54 percent) than in those cases where the aggrieved party was Jewish (44 percent).

In general, a defendant had either an appointed public defender (35 percent of defendants) or a paid lawyer (52 percent of defendants). Only 12 percent of defendants had both types of lawyer. We can characterize the various types of trials. The ratio of paid lawyers was higher than the sample average in cases related to wartime acts committed against Jews and non-Jews. The ratio was average in the ideological trials, while appointed public defenders were more typical in the other types of cases.

We now turn to the type of lawyer according to the demographics of defendants.[67] We found an overrepresentation of appointed public defenders in cases with defendants in the youngest age group. An average distribution was recorded among middle-aged defendants, while the ratio of paid lawyers was higher than average among defendants in the oldest age group. As we had expected, we found a correlation be-

---

67 In view of the low number of the mixed type (14 defendants), we will limit our analysis to those defendants with only a public appointed defender and those with only a paid lawyer.

tween the presence of a paid lawyer and the level of education and position in society of a defendant: those defendants with a better education and with higher social status were more likely than average to have only paid lawyers. Indeed, the deviation was notable, particularly concerning social status. Interestingly, there was no correlation with membership in the Arrow Cross Party or an associated organization.

Both the judges and the lawyers[68] were male, which created a special situation for a gendered analysis of the people's tribunals. We examine this issue in a separate chapter.

Characteristics of the People's Tribunal Cases

The length of trials and the number of hearings

On average, trials held by the people's tribunals ran for two years and three months. However, the various types of trial differ significantly in this regard. The average duration of cases related to wartime acts against Jews and non-Jews was two-and-a-half years. Cases related to Arrow Cross membership lasted for an average of two years. Here we found a clear difference between cases related to wartime acts and cases related to postwar acts. On average the latter were shorter by one year. The shortest cases were the ideological trials, which indicates not only that the tribunals made great efforts in this field but also that the investigation of wartime acts was a longer and more bureaucratic process, requiring a systematic approach on the part of the tribunals. However, based on micro-analysis of several cases, we also know that delays at the tribunals were due to institutional failures, defendant obstructionism, or case overload (Pető 2009a). This fact contradicts the claim made by some that these were "only" show trials. Even so, in the fluid situation after World War II, much could, and did, change in the space of two-and-a-half years. Even where a case was launched in 1945, by the time it was completed, the country had become very different politically, having fallen under communist rule. Furthermore, over time, the laws governing the people's tribunals were altered on several occasions. Unsurprisingly, we found that cases with multiple defendants

---

68   We found just one woman lawyer in the cases surveyed.

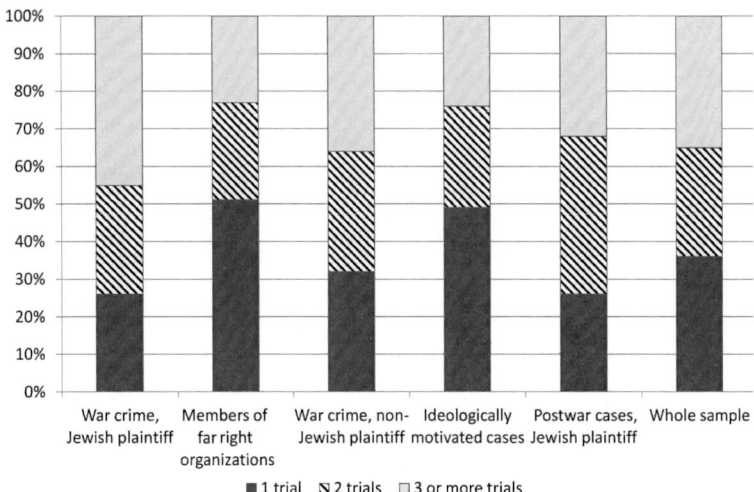

Figure 4.20 Number of hearings in the whole sample and by trial types

tended to last longer. There were multiple defendants in most cases related to wartime acts against Jews, and so these cases tended to last longer than average. However, given the scarcity of cases with multiple defendants, we could not determine—for each type of case—the presence or absence of a correlation between the number of defendants and the length of a trial.

Overall, there were roughly equal percentages of trials with one, two, and three or more hearings. We found an overrepresentation of trials with a single hearing among cases related to Arrow Cross membership and among the ideological trials: in both instances, there was a single hearing in around 50 percent of the trials. In cases related to wartime acts against Jews, we found that trials with two hearings were more likely than average: 45 percent of trials in such cases had two hearings. The same figure was 41 percent in cases related to acts committed against Jews in the postwar period.

The role of witnesses at the people's tribunals

In an earlier chapter we presented the demographics of witnesses. Now we seek to characterize witnesses based on their role in the trials. In the course of our analysis, we found that 20 percent of witnesses were supporting witnesses and 74 percent incriminating witnesses. For 6 percent of witnesses, we could not decide either way ("neutral" witnesses).

In cases related to wartime acts against Jews, we found roughly the same ratios. In cases related to membership in the Arrow Cross or an associated organization, there was a slightly higher proportion of supporting witnesses (28 percent) than the average for the whole sample. This was apparently the only type of case where this was so. The share of "neutral" witnesses was slightly higher than average (9 percent) in cases related to acts committed against non-Jews. In cases related to postwar acts, we found an overrepresentation of incriminating witnesses.

Examining the demographics of witnesses, we found an overrepresentation of supporting witnesses among witnesses in the oldest age group and among those of high social status. Meanwhile, incriminating witnesses were overrepresented among the younger age groups (particularly the middle-aged) and among working-class witnesses.

In what follows, we examine the relationship between the demographics and social status of defendants and the proportions of supporting and incriminating witnesses. Regarding defendants in the oldest age group, we found that one-quarter of witnesses were supporting witnesses. For defendants in the youngest age group, the corresponding ratio was 20 percent, while it was 16 percent in the case of middle-aged defen-

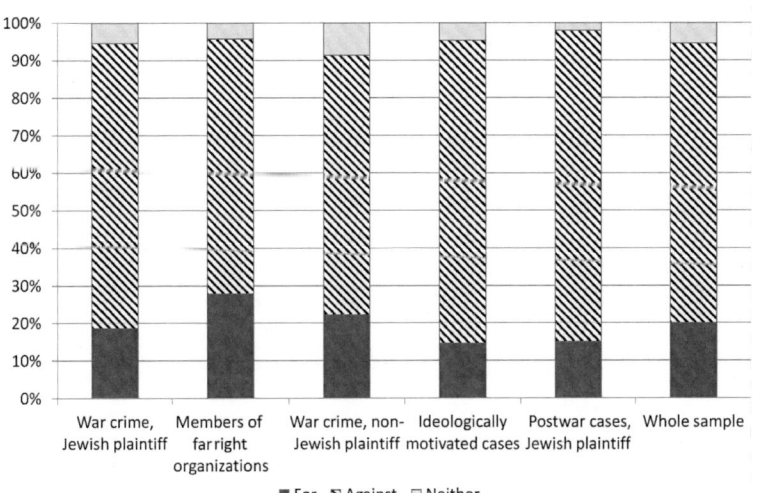

Figure 4.21 Ratios of supporting and incriminating witnesses in the whole sample and by trial types

dants. We found a positive correlation between the level of education of a defendant and the proportion of supporting witnesses. While this ratio was only 14 percent for defendants with no educational qualifications, it was 31 percent for those with university degrees. We also saw a linear correlation with the social status of defendants: where a defendant was working class or lower middle class, 18 percent of witnesses were supporting witnesses, whereas one-third of witnesses were supporting witnesses where a defendant belonged to the social elite. Defendants who were dependents (often women) were in the worst position in this respect. In their case, only 13 percent of witnesses were supporting witnesses.

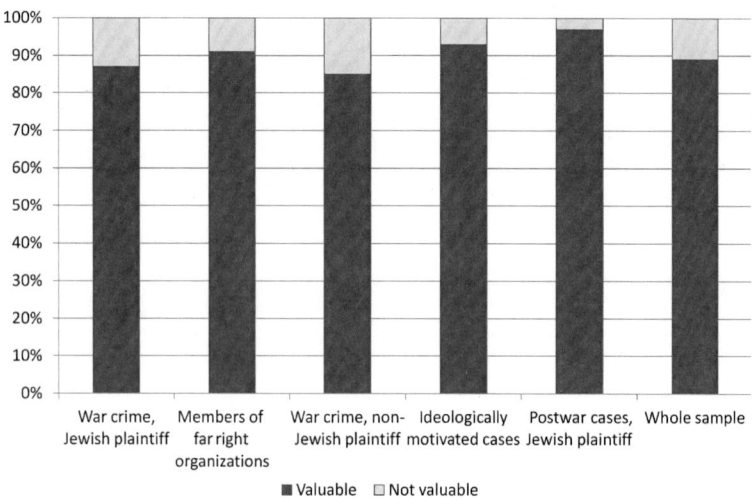

Figure 4.22 Ratios of valuable and not valuable statements in the whole sample and by trial types

We also found that the presence of a paid lawyer correlated with a higher proportion of supporting witnesses: the ratio was 21 percent for defendants with paid lawyers but only 15 percent for those with appointed public defenders. Given the small sample size, we should be cautious about drawing conclusions, but it seems that the presence of a paid lawyer particularly increased the ratio of supporting witnesses where a defendant was of low social status. Indeed, where a defendant was working class, the proportion of supporting witnesses was 13 percent when there was an appointed public defender, but 22 percent when there was a paid lawyer. Dependents were the other group for whom the presence of a paid lawyer elicited a significant increase in the ratio of supporting witnesses. In the case of such defendants, only 3 percent of witnesses were supporting witnesses when there was no paid lawyer,[69] but the ratio jumped to 18 percent when a paid lawyer was present. In the other social status groups, however, we found no correlation between the ratio of supporting witnesses and the presence or absence of a paid lawyer. This was particularly striking in the case of the elite group: although, as we have already noted, defendants in that group tended to have a higher ratio of supporting witnesses, the presence of a paid lawyer had no influence on this. It would seem, therefore, that the social status of such defendants was sufficient in itself to ensure a higher ratio of supporting witnesses.

We also classified witnesses according to whether their statements were valuable or worthless to the case. This required us to study the case files in considerable detail. We categorized a witness statement as worthless in the following typical instances: sometimes a witness would give a statement on some matter other than the case at hand. This might be because the tribunal had mistakenly called the witness to the hearing or because matters that had previously been dealt with together were now being heard separately. Sometimes witnesses would be called who then admitted they knew nothing about the case. We also classified a witness statement as worthless where the witness "knew" something based only on hearsay—for instance, on what he or she had been told by another witness. However, if such a statement was based on more than mere rumor, then we classified it as valuable. Based on our analysis, we found that 89 percent of witness statements were valuable, while 11 percent were worthless. In this respect, we observed significant differences between the various types of cases. In cases related to postwar acts, the proportion of valuable witness statements was very high. This was especially true of cases with Jewish aggrieved parties: 97 percent of witness statements in such cases were valuable. In cases related to wartime acts against Jews or to Arrow Cross membership, we observed an average distribution, while in cases related to acts committed against non-Jews, worthless witness statements were slightly overrepresented.

---

69   It should be noted that there were only 20 witnesses in this group.

We found no fundamental correlations between whether a statement was valuable and the demographics of either defendants or witnesses. Nor was there any correlation in this respect with the presence/absence of a paid lawyer.

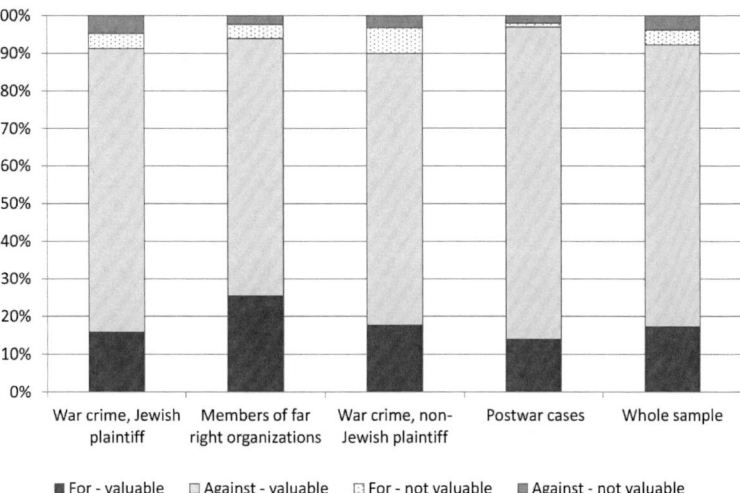

Figure 4.23 Two-dimensional typology of statements in the whole sample and by trial types

Let us now examine the co-occurrence of the two factors under analysis.[70] Three-quarters of witnesses participating in the trials made valuable statements against defendants (corroborative statements). The proportion of such statements was even higher (83 percent) in cases related to postwar acts. The proportion of witness statements that were valuable and made in support of defendants was 17 percent. In cases related to Arrow Cross membership, we found an overrepresentation of such witness statements: 25 percent of them were valuable and made in support of defendants. Worthless statements—around 8 percent of all statements—were divided almost equally between supporting statements and corroborating statements. In cases related to acts committed against non-Jews, we found a slightly higher proportion of witness statements that were supporting statements but were not valuable to the trial.

---

70 In view of the small number of cases, we only analyze the categories "supporting/corroborating" and "valuable/worthless."

In around 30 percent of cases, there was at least one witness who was not called to a hearing despite this being requested by the defense. The observed percentage was higher in cases related to wartime acts against Jews (40 percent) and lower in cases related to Arrow Cross membership (20 percent). Both in cases related to acts committed against non-Jews and in cases relating to postwar acts, the percentage was no higher than the average for the whole sample.

Examining the demographics,[71] we find that among defendants with higher educational qualifications and a higher social status, it was more likely[72] than average for there to have been a witness whose presence was requested by the defense but denied by the tribunal. It would seem that in such cases there was a relatively active defense with many witnesses, whereby the tribunal's rejection of a particular witness was more likely than otherwise.

In cases related to membership in the Arrow Cross Party or other right-wing organization,[73] the tribunal's rejection of witnesses requested by the defense occurred slightly more often than it did in the whole sample. This is especially interesting if we think back to our analysis of the number of witnesses by the type of trial, in which we found a slightly lower than average number of witnesses in such cases.

Judgments

For 63 percent of defendants, the trial was concluded by a lower court. For 37 percent of them, the case went to appeal. In this respect, we found no significant difference between the various types of cases.

When evaluating the people's tribunals, most researchers assess their efficiency in terms of the number of judgments and the rate of acquittals. In this regard, we can state that 43 percent of defendants were convicted, while 43 percent of them were acquitted. In 6 percent of cases, the judgment was a partial acquittal. A further 3 percent of defendants were placed in the "other" category. In most instances, this meant that

---

71 If a witness was asked by the defendant to give evidence but the court did not allow him or her to participate, we recorded it as an attribute of the case rather than as a characteristic of the defendant. For this reason, when seeking to analyze defendants on the basis of their demographic characteristics or their membership in the Arrow Cross, we can only consider cases with a single defendant.
72 In view of the low number of cases, we must be cautious about drawing conclusions.
73 Here we did not include the Volksbund among the Arrow Cross organizations. If the Volksbund is included in the category, there is no difference between members and non-members.

proceedings had been halted (for instance, upon the death of a defendant). Data concerning judgments and sentences were absent in 5 percent of cases. Based on all this, we may state that almost half of all cases ended in the defendant's acquittal, a very high proportion. This shows that in many instances the justice system was not functioning properly and systematically: either the trials were poorly prepared, or the wrong defendants were being brought before the tribunal.

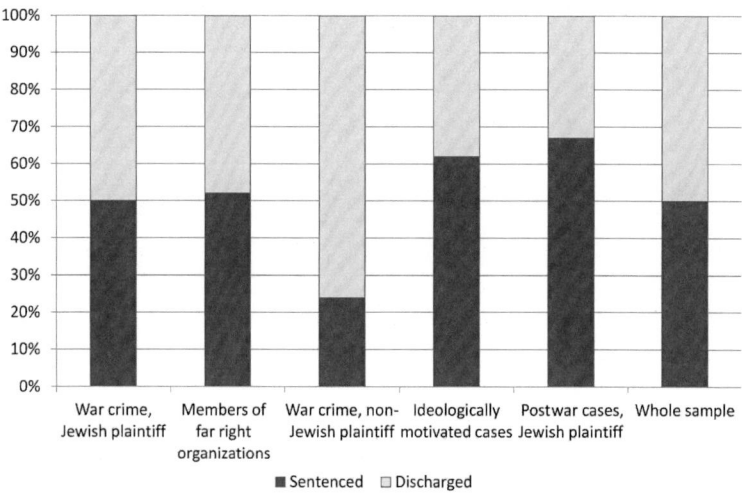

Figure 4.24 Acquittals and convictions in the whole sample and by trial types

Leaving aside the partial acquittals, we established an acquittal-conviction ratio of approximately 1:1.[74] This was the ratio in cases related to wartime acts against Jews and in cases related to Arrow Cross membership. On the other hand, the incidence of acquittals was far greater in cases related to acts committed against non-Jews, with three out of four defendants being acquitted. The acquittal ratio was lower than the sample average in cases related to postwar acts, but even here it was still around one-third.

In the cases surveyed, 12 defendants were sentenced to death at first instance, and four of these defendants then received a death sentence in the final judgment. In another case, the sentence at first instance was

---

74 In view of the low number of cases in the other categories, we shall use this breakdown on several occasions in the following.

forced labor, but the defendant was subsequently sentenced to death in the final judgment.

There were three types (or gradations) of imprisonment. The most moderate was the minimum-security prison,[75] followed by penitentiary and then maximum-security prison. A minimum-security-prison sentence was received in the final judgment by 13 percent of convicted defendants. Most such cases were already decided at the first instance. This form of punishment was less typically employed in cases that went to appeal: only 4 percent of those convicted on appeal received this sentence. The most common sentence in final judgments (70 percent of the sentences) was penitentiary. We observed this ratio in final judgments made at the first instance and on appeal. The shortest penitentiary sentence was six months; one in four penitentiary sentences were of this length. Overall, 54 percent of penitentiary sentences were for one year or less, while almost one in four were for one to two years. Only 3 percent of penitentiary sentences were for more than five years, while the longest sentence was 10 years. Maximum-security-prison sentences were relatively rare: only 3 percent (nine defendants) received such a sentence.

None of the defendants in our survey were interned. We know from the literature (Lukács 1979) that acquitted defendants were sometimes interned after the completion of a trial. However, this is not shown in the formal sentence records. Forced labor appears in 6 percent of the final judgments. Monetary fines were not imposed, but the confiscation of assets was a relatively common punishment, imposed on 18 percent of convicted defendants. Of course, we do not know whether such sentences were actually implemented. In a similar percentage of cases, the sentence included the loss of job or public office. The suspension of political rights was a general punishment. As we have shown above, this was due to legislation adopted at the time.

All five death sentences and 19 forced labor sentences were imposed in the final judgments as punishment for wartime acts. This is true despite the fact that Act VII of 1946, which served as the basis for the judgment of postwar acts, contained both types of sentence. We pointed out earlier on that minimum-security-prison sentences were abolished un-

---

75 Low-security-prison sentences were removed from among the possible sentences by the First Amendment to the PMDPJ, but the same type of sentence was reinstated by Act VII of 1946 for cases of incitement that were heard by the people's tribunals.

der the Second Amendment to the PMDPJ but that this type of sentence was reintroduced under Act VII of 1946. We see that minimum-security-prison sentences were imposed in many cases related to postwar acts. Indeed, in such cases, they accounted for 52 percent of sentences. A penitentiary sentence was imposed in 77 percent of cases related to wartime acts and in 37 percent of cases related to postwar acts.

In any appraisal of sentencing, it would be interesting to analyze the extent to which punishments were commensurate with offenses and to identify other factors influencing the sentencing process. The question arises: were certain socio-demographic groups advantaged or disadvantaged in trials held by the people's tribunals? We may suppose, for instance, that the defendants of higher social status were more likely to have had the material and other resources to achieve mitigated judgments and sentences. Furthermore, an evaluation of the case files produced by the people's tribunals—especially the ideological ones dating from the postwar period—may reveal types of cases where the offense committed by the defendant does not seem to bear any relation to the punishment. In such cases, we may suppose that the trial was a show trial. To investigate these issues, however, we need to ensure that we have "control figures"—to use a methodological term—for particular offenses. In other words, our task is to examine whether the above suppositions hold true in the case of an offense of the same gravity. For example, we can only state with certainty that a defendant of high social status has a better chance of acquittal or a lighter sentence if we can compare defendants of both low and high social status who have been charged with offenses of the same gravity. This condition, however, cannot be fulfilled for at least four interrelated reasons. First, the indictments and charges appearing in the documents are often very imprecise. For example, they often merely cite a provision of law. The legislation governing the people's tribunals includes many provisions which, in their sub-points, feature offenses of differing gravity. The second reason—which is linked with the first—lies in the number of case files included in our investigation. If we only consider those cases where the indictments/charges are clearly understood, then we will have far too few examples of the various types for a proper analysis. The third problem is that we have no clear basis for comparing the gravity of two offenses. A point of departure could be, for instance, the maximum possible sentences for the given offenses. However, in view of the legislative changes, these were altered significantly on several occasions during the period. Moreover, various sentences were featured for the same offense, the imposition of which depended on several factors. An additional problem is that in many cases the defendant was accused of a number of different offenses. The fourth reason is that we cannot know whether the indictment was correct and the defendant really did perpetrate the alleged crime. In most cases this would have been difficult to establish with accuracy even at the time of the trials; retrospectively, we clearly cannot be certain. There are, of course, a few cases where there is little doubt about a defendant's guilt, but in other cases the indictment seems to have been conjecture at best. A statistical investigation of correlations would require the use of a quantitative research program, but such a program cannot cope with the uncertainty surrounding the indictments. In other words, in our analysis, other than providing information on the distribution of the various types of judgment, we could only offer conjecture and opinion.

Women tried by the people's tribunal were more likely than men to be acquitted. This doubtless reflects the fact that women tended to have been accused of less serious and less violent crimes. Defendants with less than eight grades of education were more likely to be convicted than the average for the sample, while university graduates were more likely to be acquitted. Indeed, 65 percent of defendants in the latter group were acquitted, compared with 50 percent of the whole sample. The acquittal rate for defendants without higher educational qualifications was around the average, but this appears to have been due to two conflicting influences. While those with less education were more likely to be convicted, in the same group we also found an overrepresentation of women—who, in turn, were more likely than average to be acquitted. Only in the case of men do we see a strong correlation: those with few educational qualifications were more likely than average to be convicted. An investigation of the social status of defendants confirmed what we had found in our analysis of defendants of different gender and educational level: those of lower social status were more likely to be convicted than those of higher social status.[76] Our findings concerning women are echoed in the observation that dependents were more likely than the sample average to be acquitted.

---

76 The low number of defendants belonging to the elite means that we find no difference here, but the described relationship can be seen among middle-class defendants.

Effect of the composition of witnesses on judgments

In this part, we seek to identify the factors influencing the conviction or acquittal of defendants. Of course, when evaluating the results, we must bear in mind that the methodology has its limits—as outlined above.

If we analyze cases resulting in acquittals or convictions in terms of the number of witnesses and the ratio of supporting/incriminating witnesses, then we soon discover a rather self-evident correlation. The proportion of supporting witnesses was significantly higher (81 percent) in cases resulting in convictions than in cases resulting in acquittals (67 percent). Where a defendant was acquitted, we found a higher-than-average ratio of supporting witnesses. Indeed, in cases resulting in acquittals, on average 25 percent of witnesses were supporting witnesses. In cases resulting in convictions, the corresponding figure was only 14 percent.[77]

A very different picture emerged when we examined the same issue by type of case. In cases related to wartime acts against Jews, the judgments only seemed to depend on the proportion and number of supporting witnesses: the average ratio of supporting witnesses was significantly higher (82 percent) in cases resulting in convictions than in cases resulting in acquittals (74 percent). Similarly, the number of witnesses was also higher in cases resulting in convictions: there were, on average, eight corroborative witnesses in cases resulting in convictions and five such witnesses in cases resulting in acquittals. On the other hand, we also found that the number and proportion of supporting witnesses had no effect on the outcome of a trial. It seems, therefore, that the decisive factor in terms of the final judgment was the number of incriminating witnesses, while the presence and number of supporting witnesses was not significant.

In cases related to membership in the Arrow Cross or an associated organization, we discovered why we had been correct to record both the proportion and number of supporting/incriminating witnesses. For in these cases we found that the proportion of incriminating witnesses

---

[77] The percentages of supporting and incriminating witnesses do not add up to 100, because we only considered those witnesses who were clearly supporting or clearly incriminating. Thus if, for instance, the share of incriminating witnesses has a significant effect on a judgment, this does not necessarily mean that we shall find the same with regard to supporting witnesses. In other words, the effect of the two factors can be interpreted seperately.

was significant but that their number was not. We could deduce from this that, to a defendant, the presence of incriminating witnesses was only problematical when the proportion of such witnesses was high (in other words, when there were relatively few supporting witnesses).

In cases related to acts committed against non-Jews, we came to a different conclusion. In such cases the number or proportion of incriminating witnesses was not significant. The averages were the same both for cases resulting in acquittals and for cases resulting in convictions. On the other hand, in this type of case the proportion of supporting witnesses was significant. Indeed, we found that the proportion of supporting witnesses was 36 percent in cases resulting in acquittals but only 13 percent in cases resulting in convictions. Thus for this type of case, the effect seemed to be the opposite from what we found in cases related to acts committed against Jews. Here the factor influencing the final judgment was not the mere presence of supporting witnesses but whether the defense lawyer managed to gather a sufficient number of supporting witnesses.

In cases related to postwar acts, we found that the outcome of a trial was not affected by the ratio of supporting/incriminating witnesses. In such ideological trials it seems that the statements of witnesses simply did not count; other factors determined the fate of the defendants.

A Gendered Analysis of Political Justice in Hungary in the Aftermath of World War II

According to the literature on political justice, most convictions in Hungary were handed down to members of the former political elite and to the mostly male perpetrators of acts of violence. Hence the general history of the people's tribunals is usually presented in the form of an analysis of cases involving men. Meanwhile, some researchers in Hungary have analyzed individual court cases and have drawn, on the basis of their analysis, generalized conclusions on the operation of post-World War II justice from a gendered perspective. However, an analysis of the individual court cases of female concentration camp guards cannot tell us how the justice system functioned in terms of gender (Paul 2002; Eschebach 2003).

The feminist critique of political justice first asks: "Where were the women?" In doing so, it draws attention to the mechanisms that led to the exclusion of women. It then asks: "Where is gender in transitional justice?" This latter question "addresses the deeper conceptual exclusion of women in transitional justice projects" (Bell and O'Rourke 2007, 23). The approach we use in this chapter is a novel one, because our innovative methodology permits us both to draw conclusions regarding Hungarian political justice as a whole and to compare the different experiences of men and women within this process. In this way we can reveal the systematic emergence of masculinities and femininities in the post-World War II political justice process.

As to the question "Where were the women?" the answer is simple: women were excluded from law school until 1945. The only exceptions were a number of women who were admitted to law school at the time of the Károlyi government in 1918 and who received special permission to complete their studies. In 1928, one of these women, Margit Ungár, became the first female lawyer in Budapest to be admitted to the Bar Association; she was followed by Lili Gáspár in 1931. Another woman in this group, Erzsébet Koncz, found an occupation in the social field in Kecskemét. After 1945 Koncz was appointed as a public prosecutor for the people's tribunals (see Pető 2012). She was the only woman lawyer in our sample. This fact demonstrates how the legal profession was still almost exclusively a male one; thus an analysis of masculinities could be our task (see Hammer 2007). Consequently, in this chapter we move beyond this issue and examine the extent to which the justice mechanisms operated differently depending on whether a man or a woman was the defendant. Did the gender of a defendant make a difference in the course of a trial? Besides female defendants, there was a second group of women in the people's tribunals: the women delegated by the political parties as people's judges. This chapter also looks in detail at this group of women. In the summary we examine how gender was a factor in the treatment of war criminals and how it influenced the functioning of the people's tribunals.

Women in Political Justice: Stereotypes and Reality about Women Perpetrators

In the 500 cases surveyed, 617 defendants were brought before the court. We do not know how those appearing before the court related to war criminals overall, but the data clearly show which perpetrators were "singled out" by the political justice system. In historical collective memory and among historians too, war crimes are associated with men. Indeed, we usually think of the military officers, government ministers, and military guards (of peasant or working-class background) of the Hungarian interwar political system, the Horthy regime. In fact, however, 18 percent of such defendants were women (see Barna and Pető 2007, and Pető 2009b). This fact disproves the view that there were no female war criminals. We have already mentioned the differences between the various types of cases. Basically we found that women were underrepresented among defendants accused of crimes committed during wartime and overrepresented among those accused of crimes committed in the postwar period.

The percentage of women defendants corresponds roughly with the female participation rate in Hungarian public life, in the political parties, and in the Hungarian parliament—in the postwar period. Prior to

1945, however, only a very small percentage of women had been active in public life, and so, relatively speaking, the female defendant rate is rather high. In Hungary, the female share of criminals rose steadily in the 20th century, from 3 percent in 1900 to 10 percent in 1990. Today it is as high as 16 percent. It was during World War II that politically active women and armed women in uniform appeared for the first time in large numbers in Hungary's public sphere.

One reason for the absence of female war criminals from historical memory is a characteristic gendered feature, namely that after World War II and with the end of "the matriarchy born in need," tough action was taken in public against those women violating the patriarchal norms. However, in the post-1945 public discourse, ordinary robbers, looters, and killers, as well as the female family members of party members, did make an appearance because they fit into the public discourse that sought to restore the male-dominated social order upset by the war, while pointing out problems of exceptionality (see Pető 2009b).

The other fallacy is that these female war criminals were young and misguided. In line with the historical canon, women who were war criminals and Arrow Cross supporters—"more famous" women like the wife of Szálasi (Hungary's quisling) or the well-known actress Sári Fedák—do feature in the historical account. This serves to support the misconception that most of the female party members were middle-class or lower-middle-class women who, lacking their own professional aspirations, had become Arrow Cross members at the instigation of male relatives (husbands and fathers) and who, having become members, kept a low public profile. A further possible explanation for women's invisibility might be that, in addition to misguided women and those subject to male manipulation, sadistic, psychopathic women became Arrow Cross members.

The empirical data, however, revealed something quite different. The average age of the women perpetrators was 38 years. If we look at the full age distribution, a striking feature is the predominance of those aged 30–49 (in 1945). While 56 percent of women defendants were aged 30–49, the census data[78] indicate that only 36 percent of the general population fell in this age group. The share of younger women (those aged

---

78   When analyzing the women and men, we relate the figures not to the general population but rather to the distribution of women and men according to the various socio-demographic variables within the general population.

30 or under in 1945) corresponds approximately to their share of the general population, whereas older people were underrepresented among defendants (16 percent of defendants, compared with 38 percent for the whole population). In terms of the age distribution, we found no difference between male and female defendants.[79]

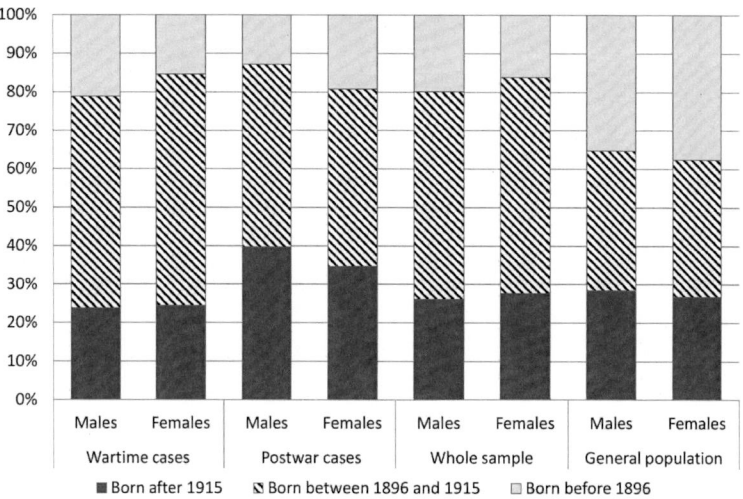

Figure 5.1 Age distribution of defendants by gender and by the time of crime; gender and age distribution of the general population

Regardless of whether the crimes were committed during wartime or in the postwar period,[80] the age distribution of female defendants is the same in a statistical sense.[81] Among male defendants, however, a significant difference may be observed: younger men (those aged 30 or under) are overrepresented in cases related to postwar acts. Younger defendants had typically shouted abuse—possibly while drunk—in public places, whereas the middle-aged group were those who had taken part in the anti-Jewish wartime atrocities. Thus it cannot be claimed that the perpetrators acted out of hotheadedness or without thinking. On the

---

79 In 1930, men and women in the general population had a similar age distribution. The current difference in the age distribution of men and women is largely the result of the selective (gender-related) effect of the war. This has added to the effect of the growing difference in male and female life expectancy.
80 In view of the small sample size, we cannot compare the various types of cases. Thus in this chapter of the book, we limit our analysis to a comparison of cases related to wartime acts with cases related to postwar acts.
81 It is likely, however, that among female defendants too, the middle-aged are overrepresented for the wartime cases, while the younger age group is overrepresented for crimes committed during the postwar period. This difference, however, is not large enough for the two figures to differ in a statistical sense.

contrary, the women and men who chose to steal, murder, blackmail, and plunder were well established and integrated in the fabric of society.

The third question concerns the type of settlement in which the women defendants were born. The data indicate an overrepresentation of women born in rural areas. Whereas according to the census data, 48 percent of the general population were born in rural areas, the corresponding percentage for female defendants was 59 percent. In this regard, we found no difference between male and female defendants. Thus those who exploited the discriminatory legal framework to enrich themselves were typically people who had moved to Budapest from rural areas rather than natives of the city. Having broken away from their previous social networks, such people became supporters of the extremist political movements.

The fourth question concerns the education level of defendants. A striking finding is that women defendants were significantly better educated than women in the general population. Whereas 12 percent of women in the general population had an eighth-grade education and 2 percent had a high school diploma, the corresponding percentages among the female defendants were 23 percent and 6 percent.

Male defendants were also typically more educated than the general population. An important difference, however, can be observed in the structure of the discrepancy. Among male defendants we found a smaller percentage—smaller than in the general population—of people who had attended school but had not completed eight grades and a significantly larger percentage of people with a high school diploma or a college or university degree. Whereas 8 percent of men aged 20 or over in the general population had a high school diploma and 3 percent had a college or university degree, the corresponding figures for the male defendants were 19 percent and 14 percent. People with less than an eighth-grade education were also significantly underrepresented among the female defendants, but here the real "surplus" was found not at the top of the educational hierarchy but in its middle section: whereas 12 percent of women aged 20 or over in the general population had completed eight grades of education, this was the level of education of 23 percent of female defendants.

In view of the distribution of defendants by level of education, it cannot be claimed that those with the least education were more likely to be anti-Semites or "misguided." Similarly, it is impossible to argue that Arrow Cross rule was "mob" rule whereby people at the bottom of

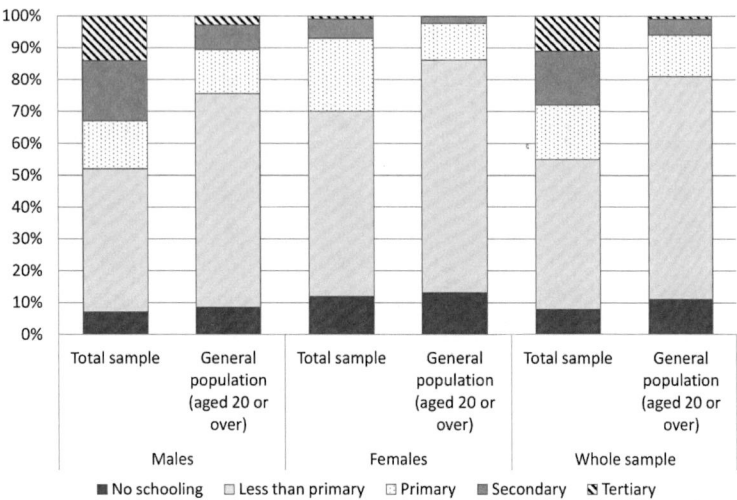

Figure 5.2 Educational level of defendants in the whole sample and by gender; age and educational level of the general population aged 20 or over

society sought to gain from the social turmoil and did not shy away from violence. One can also refute the claim that the better educated found it easier to avoid being held responsible or that they were the young people who were inclined to emigrate and who fled westwards with the German troops in order to escape the Red Army.

The fifth question concerns the political activity/involvement of defendants. Thirty-six percent of the female defendants accused of wartime crimes had been members of the Arrow Cross or an associated organization. If we also include membership in the Volksbund—which had many women members as a result of its recruitment policy—then this figure increases to 46 percent. The percentages were higher—51 and 59 percent—among male defendants. This shows that Arrow Cross membership was not an essential condition for committing acts of physical violence or abuse.

Witnesses

Twenty-six percent of witnesses were women. Examining the age of female witnesses, as we did for all witnesses, we found an overrepresentation of the middle-aged (those aged 30–49 in 1945): while 36 percent of the general population belonged in this age group, the figure was 57 percent for female witnesses. The percentages for the youngest and oldest age groups are smaller than in the general population. Whereas in the census figures 27 percent of women were aged under 30 and 38 percent were aged 50 or over in 1945, in our sample the figures for both age groups were 22 and 21 percent. Comparing the age distribution of female defendants with the distribution for males, one can see higher percentages of older people among the males (21 percent for women, 26 percent for men), while the middle-aged are overrepresented among females (57 percent among women, 53 percent among men).

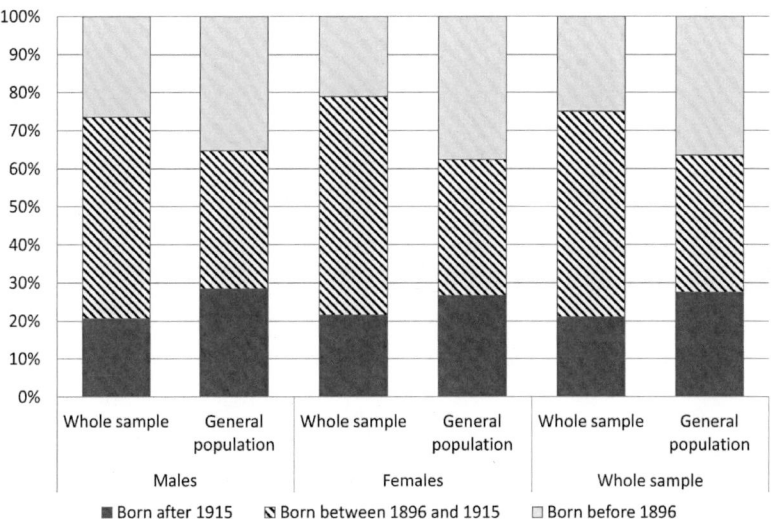

Figure 5.3 Age distribution of witnesses in the whole sample and by gender; gender and age distribution of the general population

Women defendants were more likely than women in the general population to have been born in Budapest: 28 percent of female defendants were natives of Budapest, compared with 17 percent of women in the general population. Inhabitants of urban areas outside Budapest were slightly underrepresented in comparison with the general population, while the percentage of rural inhabitants was roughly equal. In this regard, we found no difference between male and female defendants.

Court Judgments

Regarding the ratio of cases that went to appeal, we only found a difference between female and male defendants when we distinguished between cases related to wartime acts and cases related to postwar acts. Seventy-two percent of cases involving female defendants accused of wartime crimes were decided by the People's Tribunal at first instance, while 28 percent of such cases went to appeal. Among male defendants the percentage of cases going to appeal was somewhat higher: 39 percent. In cases related to postwar acts, a slightly higher number of appeals were made by female defendants; here 36 percent of cases were decided on appeal. In this area, similar percentages were observed for male defendants.

54 percent of women defendants were acquitted, while 31 percent were convicted and 14 percent received partial acquittals. A smaller proportion of male defendants were acquitted: 44 percent were fully acquitted, 5 percent were partially acquitted, and the remaining 48 percent were convicted. The above difference between female and male defendants was seen both in cases related to wartime acts and in cases related to postwar acts; the difference, however, varied. The disparity in the ratio of full acquittals was relatively small in cases related to wartime acts: 55 percent of female defendants and 46 percent of male defendants received full acquittals in such cases. In such cases, however, we found a significantly higher percentage of partial acquittals among female defendants: whereas 16 percent of women defendants were partially acquitted, the corresponding figure among male defendants was only 5 percent. Meanwhile, male defendants were significantly more likely to be convicted: 44 percent of male defendants were convicted, compared with 28 percent of females. In cases related to postwar acts, 52 percent of female defendants received full acquittals. This percentage was significantly higher than the figure for men (30 percent). Moreover, in cases of this type, male defendants were far more likely to be found guilty: 68 percent of them received convictions, compared with 41 percent of the women. In general, therefore, the acquittal rate was higher among women defendants. There are two possible reasons for this. Either the women committed less serious crimes and so were rightfully acquitted in larger numbers, or they received more moderate sentences for crimes that were otherwise of similar gravity.

The above reasoning—that women either perpetrated less serious crimes or were subject to less strict sentencing—implies that less severe forms of punishment should be more common for their group, but this is not what we found. A penitentiary sentence was the most common form of punishment for both women and men, although such a sentence was received by 64 percent of women compared with 72 percent of men. Examining the lesser and more severe forms of punishment, however, we made an interesting finding: minimum-security-prison sentences were more common among female defendants. Whereas 19 percent of women (8 of 29 convicted women) were sentenced to detention at a minimum-security prison, the corresponding figure for men was 12 percent. Regarding maximum-security-prison sentences, we encountered the problem of a low sample size, for—as already noted—there were only nine defendants who received this type of sentence. This means we should be cautious about drawing conclusions. At any rate, we can state that three of the nine defendants receiving maximum-security-prison sentences were women, whereas the female ratio of convicted defendants was only 15 percent.

Sentences received by women typically took the form of a fine or the confiscation of assets:[82] this was the form of punishment for 27 percent of the convicted women (13 of 45 convicted women) but for only 18 percent of men.

We turn now to the length of sentences.[83] In line with the above logic, here too we expected to find that, on average, women received shorter sentences. In fact, however, the length of sentences for women and men was about the same, with an average sentence of 20 months (almost two years). If, instead of the length of sentences, we examine the other categories analyzed earlier on, then we find almost the same ratios for both male and female defendants.

Women People's Judges

In the 500 cases surveyed, a total of 1,076 hearings took place. In 23 percent of the hearings, there was at least one female people's judge. We found that there were two years in the period under investigation when the percentage of hearings with female people's judges differed significantly from the

---

[82] Of the two types of punishment, the latter had a significantly higher incidence.
[83] We can only examine this aspect in the case of penitentiary sentences, because in that area we have a sufficient amount of data.

average for the whole sample. In 1947, 33 percent of hearings had at least one female people's judge, while the figure for 1948 was only 19 percent. As regards the various types of cases, we found that the percentage of hearings with female people's judges was relatively high in cases related to wartime acts against Jews (30 percent) and in cases related to membership in the Arrow Cross or an associated organization (30 percent). In cases related to postwar acts and particularly in the ideological trials, we found an underrepresentation of hearings with female people's judges. Indeed, in the ideological trials the proportion of such hearings was only 9 percent.

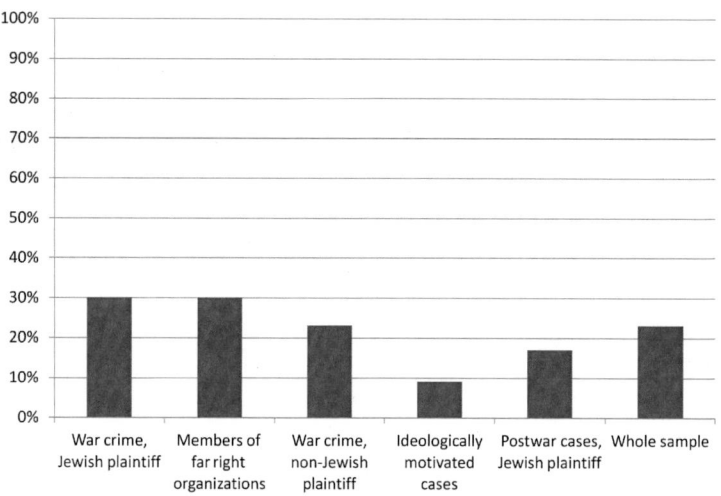

Figure 5.4 Ratios of female people's judges by trial types and in the whole sample

A total of 252 hearings included participation by female people's judges, and in all, 34 female people's judges participated. In other words, most female people's judges participated in several hearings. In the course of our analysis, we found that some of these women had been particularly active. We concluded that there must have been reasons (personal contacts, position in party hierarchy, etc.) why certain women became so active in the work of the people's tribunals.

Examining the women according to their party affiliation,[84] we were immediately struck by the significant representation of the Na-

---

84 Here we only considered those people's judges whose party affiliations were known to us. This was 98 percent of the people's judges.

tional Peasants Party *(Nemzeti Parasztpárt)*. Thirty-four percent of the female people's judges came to the Budapest People's Tribunal as delegates of that political party. Nine percent of the female people's judges were delegates sent by the Hungarian Communist Party *(Magyar Kommunista Párt)*, while 13 percent were sent by the Social Democratic Party *(Szociáldemokrata Párt)*. After these two parties merged and became the Hungarian Workers' Party *(Magyar Dolgozók Pártja)*, the share was 13 percent. This is a relatively high percentage if one considers that the party was established only in June 1948. Meanwhile, the National Trade Union Council *(Országos Szakszervezeti Tanács)* seems to have been particularly active. Even though it could delegate people's judges for only a relatively short period of time—from the entry into force of the Second Amendment to the PMDPJ until the enactment of Act XXXIV of 1947—its share of the female people's judges was 20 percent. The Independent Smallholders Party *(Független Kisgazdapárt)* delegated the smallest number of female people's judges—just 2 percent.

Six people's judges were delegated by several parties or organizations. Three of the six were initially delegated by the National Trade Union Council *(Országos Szakszervezeti Tanács)* and then—after this body's right to delegate judges was abolished—by the Hungarian Communist Party *(Magyar Kommunista Párt)* or, subsequently, by the Hungarian Workers' Party *(Magyar Dolgozók Pártja)*. The others were initially delegated by the Hungarian Communist Party *(Magyar Kommunista Párt)* and then—after its merger with the Social Democratic Party *(Szociáldemokrata Párt)*—by the Hungarian Workers' Party *(Magyar Dolgozók Pártja)*.

The large number of female judges delegated by the National Peasants Party *(Nemzeti Parasztpárt)* was one of the most significant findings of our analysis. The finding is particularly striking in view of the fact that the party only began to establish its apparatus in 1945 and was mainly active outside Budapest. The party's radical manifesto—which resembled the Hungarian Communist Party's *(Magyar Kommunista Párt)* program—included a commitment to bring the pre-1945 regime to account. Unfortunately, only part of the written records of the National Peasants Party *(Nemzeti Parasztpárt)* have survived, and so they cannot assist us in explaining this phenomenon (for more details on the party, see Pető 1998).

Summary: Gender in Political Justice

Previous research on political justice has concentrated on the status of female victims and the punishment and punishability of sexual crimes. Our research is novel in that we have examined female perpetrators, comparing them with men. In this way we have shown how political justice functions from a gender perspective. In addition, we have also examined whether women were present in the justice system. Here we found that—with the exception of the National Peasants Party *(Nemzeti Parasztpárt)*—the political parties in Hungary paid scant attention to the postwar gender equality discourse when choosing their delegates to the people's tribunals.

As far as the defendants are concerned, previous quantitative research based on individual cases had indicated that female perpetrators generally received tougher sentences than men who committed the same types of crime—unless the gender stereotypes were played out in court, whereby a female perpetrator claimed to be a "misled woman" who had committed her crime under the influence of a male relative (Pető 2009a). Our systematic quantitative research revealed the functioning of political justice. It showed that with regards to women, the justice system occupied an extreme position. This finding came as no surprise, for this was the first time that large numbers of women had been brought before the courts. Our analysis indicated that the sentencing of women was sometimes more moderate and sometimes more severe than the sentencing of men. Women were more likely to be acquitted, fined, have their assets confiscated, or detained at a minimum-security prison. Of course, one might argue that women perpetrators typically committed crimes that were more moderate than the crimes committed by men, and so they received more moderate punishment. But this does not explain the tougher sentences, for women were also more likely to be incarcerated at a maximum-security prison—the toughest sentence. Nor does it explain why women, on average, received the same length of sentence as men. Here we have reached the limits of the usefulness of quantitative research: at the next step we must return to a qualitative analysis of individual cases—doing so, however, with a clear awareness of the general picture.

Jewish Identity and the People's Tribunals

Holocaust experts agree that until the Eichmann trial, the needs of Jews as a community were ignored by the justice system, as social changes in the aftermath of war and the realities of the Cold War diverted attention from the sufferings of Jews in all European countries. There is also agreement that "Jewish survivors, indeed survivors in general, were incapable of illuminating the general picture because of a prosecution strategy that favored documents above fragile memory" (Bloxham 2004, 401). This chapter offers evidence, based on the data at our disposal, that these conclusions do not apply in Hungary, where Jewish survivors were able, in part, to realize their interests in the justice system in the immediate postwar period. One reason for this was numerical: there were around 140,000 Holocaust survivors among a total Hungarian population of 8.5 million (Braham 1994; Deák 2006, 129). Two factors contributed to the survival of Hungary's Jews. First, many Jewish men served in the unarmed labor battalions (alongside the Hungarian army) at the front, where they lived and worked amid inhuman conditions but where their chances of survival were greater than those of the deportees. The second reason was that the deportation of Jews from Budapest came to a halt in the summer of 1944. Another factor enhancing the ability of Jewish survivors to realize their interests was the high degree of assimilation of Hungary's Jews and their integration in Hungarian society. This applied in particular to the Jewish community in Budapest, who formed the majority of survivors (Karády 2002).

This chapter examines the records of the people's courts that shed light on the identity of those Jews who were aggrieved parties in trials held by the tribunals and who gave evidence about their grievances. We look at how Jews experienced the trials, how long the trials lasted, what kinds of verdicts were obtained, and who the perpetrators and the witnesses were.

The chapter also discusses two hitherto neglected aspects of postwar history: How did the system of political justice contribute to the formation of a reactive and negative identity? And how did the people's tribunals establish the language of the memory of World War II? (Pető 2007 and 2009a)

World War II was still raging in Hungary when the first trials began. At the time, the Holocaust (or Shoah) discourse was yet to begin; the world knew only of crimes—and of victims and perpetrators. And the victims expected to receive justice. We ask the question: Who controls the means of the symbolic serving of justice? It is not enough to serve justice; it must also be communicated, and this process has also an emotional element: victims need to feel that they have received justice. The chapter analyzes how the Jewish survivors lost this symbolic battle. It concludes by comparing the verdicts in cases related to crimes against Jews with the verdicts in wartime cases that were unrelated to the Holocaust. We find that the paradoxes and abnormalities of the postwar political justice process were a profound disappointment to Jewish citizens, who had placed their trust in the legalist version of retribution and had rejected lynching and other forms of violence. Moreover, not only did the system of people's tribunals fail to properly investigate and punish crimes committed against Jews, but also Jewish aggrieved parties found themselves labeled as agents of Jewish revenge while being deprived of any institutional form of collective identity formation.

Characteristics of the People's Tribunal Cases

Cases related to acts committed against Jews account for 43 percent of all cases in our research. We have already mentioned that previous researchers analyzed the process of transitional justice in Hungary by looking at individual cases. A partial exception to this approach was László Karsai's research (Karsai 2004). His research focused on the written documentation created by the Budapest People's Tribunal. Assisted by colleagues, he determined how many cases in each year during the period 1945–1949 related to Jews. In his research, he placed in this category those cases mentioning the word "Jewish" or "Jew."[85] Based on

---

[85] He initially wanted to include cases featuring the word *cigány* [Roma], but this word only occurred twice in the case files that underwent detailed analysis.

this definition, he found that 17 percent of cases belonged in this category. He also established that the ratio of such cases decreased rapidly from 1947, whereafter only 10 percent of the cases could be placed in this category. In our research, we classified the cases after a full investigation of the contents of the case files. Based on our method, we found that a far greater percentage of cases were related to acts committed against Jews.[86] Like Karsai, we also found that the share of such cases declined from 1947 onwards, but the decrease in our case was smaller. Thus we found that Jewish-related cases accounted for 55 and 47 percent of all cases in 1945 and 1946, respectively, and that the ratio had only fallen to 29 percent by 1949. The reason for this may have been the changing word usage, which reflected ongoing political changes. In the run-up to the communist takeover—and particularly after the takeover—Jews in Hungary began to be treated in line with the Soviet approach. The authorities did their utmost to eliminate the Jews as a separate group in society, and this effort was manifested even in the suppression of the word "Jewish." It seems that the records of the people's tribunals also adapted to the changing word usage. Instead of the word "Jew" or "Jewish," other, more acceptable "synonyms" were used (e.g., "persecuted"). Karsai identified case files that needed to be analyzed in detail. He limited his analysis to a single year (1946), arguing that in that year the basic procedural rules of the people's tribunals were already in place but the domestic political skirmishes had yet to begin. In 1946, there were, according to Karsai's analysis, 1,401 cases that could be classified as "Jewish cases." A further limitation in Karsai's research was his exclusion from the analysis of the trials of forced labor camp officials and guards. In his view, owing to the contradictions surrounding labor service, such cases needed to be analyzed separately. This limitation, however, meant that Karsai's 748 cases bore even less resemblance to the cases defined in our analysis as being Jewish-related (i.e., cases related to acts committed against Jews). We also identified a fundamental difference in the method of processing data. While Karsai's research included numerical data, they were based simply on enumerated calculations. Karsai's methodological apparatus did not allow for an analysis of relationships and correlations. Alongside the numerical data, he—like

---

86 This remains true even if we consider the sample error for our estimation, that is, the probable value range within which the percentages would fall if we were to examine all the case files.

previous researchers—tended to present individual cases. For all these reasons, the findings of our analysis cannot be compared with Karsai's research results, given the differences in the range of cases investigated and in the methods and approaches employed.

In our analysis, we found that cases related to wartime acts against Jews most often involved physical abuse (43 percent), unlawful material gain (32 percent), or reporting on people (32 percent). Anti-Semitic verbal abuse accounted for 13 percent of cases.[87] We also defined two other types of cases where the alleged crime was committed during wartime but where the aggrieved party seemed to have been non-Jewish (although in view of the historical context, the possibility could not be excluded that the aggrieved party was Jewish). Concerning the postwar period, one type of case included acts committed against Jews, while the other type comprised the ideological trials. Cases related to acts committed against Jews in the postwar period amounted to 7 percent of all cases. We found that in all such cases the alleged crime was verbal anti-Semitic abuse—a category of crime listed in Act VII of 1946. Evidently, anti-Jewish sentiment was being expressed verbally. Despite all the news of death camps and mass murder, anti-Semitic hate speech was still present in Hungary. The fifth type of case was the ideological trials (12 percent). Although such cases were heard by the people's tribunal, their purpose was clearly to silence the opposition.[88] We see, therefore, that the court addressed "purely" wartime crimes for less than a year. During this initial period, the court attempted—amid the ruins of war—to deal with people's complex feelings and their expectations of revenge and redress.

Historians tend to regard Act VII of 1946 as an instrument for restricting democracy in the defense of democracy, which was indeed the Act's principal aim during the coalition struggle at the beginning of the Cold War (Bernáth 1993; Gyenesei 2011). As mentioned above, the Act punished those who incited ethnic, racial, or religious hatred. A particular aim of the Act was to influence the value system of people in the postwar period by means of prescriptive legislation. A precedent for the

---

87 It should be emphasized that a defendant may have committed several types of crime. We placed such defendants in all the affected groups.
88 Some of the cases were related to crimes in the postwar period and were ideological in nature but also related to crimes against Jews. These were now placed in the category of cases related to crimes against Jews in the postwar period.

punishment of political views existed in Hungarian judicial practice. Indeed, the charge of "incitement" had been used—to little effect—as a legal instrument against people with communist views and, in the 1930s, against people with extreme right-wing views. In the few cases where the charge was made in connection with anti-Semitic verbal abuse, public memory treated it as "Jewish revenge" (Bernáth 1993, 4). One should also note that the court rarely punished anti-Semitic verbal abuse on its own but linked it with the need to defend democracy.[89]

Defendants and Their Characteristics

We described the defendants in detail in a previous chapter. Here we summarize the documentary material on cases related to acts committed against Jews. Cases related to wartime acts against Jews typically had a relatively large number of defendants. In such cases, the gender distribution of defendants was average, but we did find differences in the types of crime committed, which tended to confirm gender stereotypes. In general, cases related to postwar acts had a higher proportion of female defendants. In comparison with the census data for the general population, we found an overrepresentation of middle-class defendants, and this was true for both types of cases involving Jewish aggrieved parties. A deviation from the sample distribution was seen among defendants in cases related to acts committed against Jews in the postwar period: young people were overrepresented among such defendants. Defendants in cases related to wartime acts against Jews were more likely than the sample average to have been born in Budapest. The educational level of defendants in such cases was in line with the sample average distribution, but this was still much higher than the average education level among the general population. Analysis of the social status of defendants in cases related to wartime acts against Jews revealed an overrepresentation of lower-middle-class people among this group. Turning now to political mobilization, we found that almost half of the defendants in cases related to wartime acts against Jews had been members of the Arrow Cross Party *(Nyilaskeresztes Párt)* or an associated or-

---

[89] Of the 34 cases related to crimes against Jews in the postwar period, 11 cases exclusively involved "verbal anti-Semitic abuse."

ganization. In this regard, we identified a difference between male and female defendants: unsurprisingly, Arrow Cross membership was more common among men (52 percent) than among women (34 percent). Even so, the fact that a third of female defendants were members of the Arrow Cross Party or an associated organization is striking and indicative of the political activization of women.

Witnesses and Their Characteristics

In terms of our overall analysis, witness statements represented an important element. Before presenting our results, we should first mention several factors influencing the conclusions that have been drawn from our data. In the witness statements recorded during an investigation preceding a people's-tribunal trial, a note was made of a witness's religion (religious denomination). This piece of data was also recorded in the documents drawn up during the trial proceedings (e.g., court records). However, as time passed—and reflecting the political changes in Hungary—it became less and less common to record such data. Thus, whereas for cases launched in 1945 we know the religion of 63 percent of witnesses, for cases launched in 1946–1948 the corresponding figure is 30–40 percent, and for cases launched in 1949 it is only 20 percent. Clearly, religion was recorded in fewer and fewer cases. Given the distribution over time of the various types of cases—a distribution described above—it is evident that our knowledge of the religious affiliation of witnesses varies for the different types of cases. The ratio is highest—50 percent—for cases related to wartime acts against Jews.[90] Since we knew that religious affiliation formed a cornerstone of the Jewish aspects of our research, in our analysis of the case files we did two things in connection with the witnesses. First, we recorded whether the religious affiliation of a witness had become known during a case. In this way, we were able to establish the religious affiliation of an additional 18 percent of witnesses. This was achievable particularly in cases related to wartime acts against Jews, as this was the area where the religious affiliation of a witness was most likely to have been recorded in

---

90 Because the data deficiencies were systematic, we were unable to compare the witnesses in cases by religion.

the trial records. Furthermore, the religious affiliation of witnesses could be determined in a relatively high percentage of other cases related to wartime acts. In cases related to postwar acts, information in the case files almost never revealed the religious affiliation of witnesses. Another task was to compare the official records for religious affiliation with the religious affiliation we identified by studying the contents of the case file. Our aim here was to identify Jewish converts to Christianity as Jews, based on their experiences during the Holocaust as revealed by the contents of a case file. This procedure enabled us, with a high degree of confidence, to identify as Jews 10 percent of those persons previously recorded as non-Jews. In the course of our analysis, we will use a factor established by combining the two types of approach.

In the 215 cases related to wartime acts against Jews, there were at least 726 witnesses who were certainly Jewish[91] and an additional 87 witnesses who were probably Jewish. In our estimation, therefore, in the trials held by the Budapest People's Tribunal, approximately 27,000–36,000 Jewish witnesses took part in cases related to wartime acts against Jews.[92] This number increases to 39,000 if we include those witnesses who were probably Jewish. If we only consider the period 1945–1946—during which there were no ideological trials—then the number of Jewish witnesses was between 11,000 and 14,000—or as many as 16,000, if we also include witnesses who were probably Jewish.

In the following, we compare and contrast the demographic characteristics of Jewish and non-Jewish witnesses in cases related to wartime acts against Jews.[93] The percentage of females is higher among Jewish witnesses: 34 percent, compared with 24 percent among non-Jewish witnesses. This may well be explained by the demographic structure of

---

91 We can be sure that this is an underestimate of the total number of Jewish witnesses involved.

92 We found that 33.8 percent of witnesses in cases related to acts committed against Jews were certainly Jewish. We have mentioned several times already that this value is only an estimate and that there is a certain error percentage. This error can be calculated using statistical mathematics. In our case it is ±4.2 percent. That is to say, the real percentage is between 33.8−4.2 = 29.6 and 33.8 + 4.2 = 38.0. The total number of witnesses in cases related to acts committed against Jews can be calculated for the period as a whole; according to our estimate, it is 93,325. Thus, using the above percentages, we can state that 31,546 Jewish witnesses participated in cases related to wartime acts against Jews and that, in all likelihood, the number would be between 27,583 and 35,508 if we were to examine every single case heard by the people's tribunal.

93 Owing to the aforementioned problems, the results are not generally applicable. Nevertheless, if we assume that there is no systematic difference between the missing data for the religious affiliation of Jews and that for the religious affiliation of non-Jews, then it would seem that by analyzing the data, we can gain some impression of the participants in the proceedings.

the Jewish survivor population, for there were higher numbers of women. There was no difference in the age distribution of Jewish and non-Jewish witnesses. Among Jewish witnesses, we found an overrepresentation of people born in Budapest and an underrepresentation of people from rural areas. Each of these groups accounted for 39 percent of Jewish witnesses, whereas the figures for non-Jewish witnesses were 27 percent and 49 percent respectively. Dependents were significantly overrepresented among Jewish witnesses, and this circumstance also reflects the large number of women. Dependents accounted for 23 percent of Jewish witnesses but only 13 percent of non-Jewish witnesses. Forty percent of Jewish witnesses were middle class, while this was true of only 31 percent of non-Jewish witnesses. Among non-Jewish witnesses, we found relatively high ratios for the working class, the lower middle class, and the social elite. Indeed, among non-Jewish witnesses the ratios for these social classes were 19, 26, and 10 percent, whereas among Jewish witnesses the same ratios were 10, 22, and 6 percent.

Court Judgments

As we noted already, 58 percent of cases related to wartime acts against Jews were concluded by the people's tribunal at first instance, while 42 percent of them went to appeal. This appeal rate is slightly higher than the rate for all cases (38 percent). Based on an analysis of cases resulting in a full conviction or a full acquittal,[94] one can state that 50 percent of cases related to wartime acts against Jews resulted in acquittals. This is exactly the same figure as the percentage for all cases. Even so, an acquittal rate of 50 percent seems remarkably high and evidently had consequences.

Jewish Identity and the Practice of Political Justice

Many survivors filed charges, made witness statements, or gave testimonies to the police and to the tribunal. During the first cases heard by the people's tribunals, onlookers—many of whom were related to the

---

94 This is necessary in view of the small number of cases.

victims—were prone to interrupt the ritualized judicial proceedings. For instance, often in tears, they would ask the guards of defendants for information about missing family members (Major 1988, 122). Later on, through their attendance at hearings, survivors could see justice done and learn the legal vocabulary they needed to use when giving accounts of the atrocities to the tribunals or to their close relatives (for more on this, see Pető 2009a). There is a wealth of written material containing the frank accounts of Jewish survivors concerning the atrocities of World War II. Of course, such statements were made within the ritualized framework of the justice system.

An important role in the nascent justice system was played by lay people's judges, who, after being delegated by the five coalition parties[95] forming Hungary's government between 1945 and 1947, took part in trials of first instance. In appeal cases, professional lawyers were delegated as professional people's judges by the same parties. Following a proposal by Justice Minister István Ries, a Social Democrat, it was decided that appointees to the position of professional people's judge should not have been active under the Horthy regime of the interwar period. According to the people's judge Ákos Major, much of Hungarian society considered the people's tribunals to be instruments of Jewish revenge, particularly because people of Jewish ancestry played such a large part in their functioning (Major 1988, 187). We shall return at the end of this chapter to this structural asymmetry—"blaming the victim"—which is linked with the symbolic serving of justice.

Post-Shoah Jewish identity has been characterized as mostly negative and reactive. It was an identity that was not chosen voluntarily but was enforced on individuals by the social milieu. This identity has often been described in the literature as constituted primarily by the Holocaust (Erős 1992; Karády 1992; Kovács 1988). Of course, the Holocaust itself led some Jews to dispense with their Jewish identity. In Hungary, however, such a desire was strengthened by the social and political milieu.

When did this social and political milieu arise? Was it a byproduct of the communist takeover and the introduction of a Soviet-style policy towards Jewish identity? Or was it the result of events in the immediate

---

95 It was mentioned earlier that under the First Amendment to the PMDPJ, the National Trade Union Council *(Országos Szakszervezeti Tanács)* received the right to delegate a people's judge. This right of the Council was abolished by Act XXXIV of 1947.

aftermath of the war, including even the proceedings of the people's tribunals? Evidently, there were several obstacles to the development of a positive identity. The abrogation of Hungary's anti-Jewish laws and decrees began in 1945. Although legislation was adopted in 1946 on "the persecution of Hungarian Jews and mitigating the consequences thereof," the preamble to the law deals with the issue of responsibility in a rather contradictory manner. It claims that the survival of the Jews of Budapest was due in part to "the humanity of the Hungarian people," which offered "shining testimony that broad sections of the Hungarian people were able to remain true to human ideals despite the terror and misleading propaganda" (for the text of the law, see Gonda 1992, 302). In this way, society at large—much of which had passively observed if not actively participated in the persecution of Jews and others—was let off the hook, and Hungarian fascism was portrayed as the work of an elite clique and a criminal government. In this chapter we argue that this political rhetoric was at variance with the practice of the people's tribunals, where grievances suffered by Jews during wartime received no legal redress.

Moreover, the Jewish survivors received no financial compensation. There were reasons for this. The lack of compensation implied that society bore no responsibility for the events, while those who rightly demanded the return of their property were branded "greedy." Paradoxically, the Jews' return was more disturbing to the general population than their ghettoization and deportation had been (Pelle 1995, 151).

Political justice is just one aspect of justice; the other is financial compensation. A theory of distributive justice was elaborated by Nozick, who in his book *Anarchy, State, and Utopia* (Nozick 1974) designated a full compensation in a liberal framework as the ideal aim. In post-World War II Hungary, however, this would have been impractical in many cases. For this reason, emotional compensation, which restores the victim's self-esteem, or moral compensation, which restores moral standards, might have been more useful in terms of developing a collective memory (Tyler 2006, 19). The property of Hungary's Jewish survivors was not returned, but their civil rights were restored in full through the abrogation of the anti-Jewish laws (Pogany 1997, 155–178). Where an apartment had previously been inhabited by a Jewish family, the new residents were told that they could not prevent the return of the Jewish owners. This did little to promote peaceful coexistence (Deák 2006, 143). The Communist Party "resolved" the supply problems of the postwar period by criminalizing the black market and by proposing and then implementing the nationalization of business and industry. The battle against black-marketeers had coded anti-Semitic features, resulting in pogroms in various parts of the country in 1946. In his keynote work on the period, the liberal humanist Bibó analyzed the multifaceted problems, acknowledging that Jews' participation in the justice system and their joining the Communist Party *(Kommunista Párt)* in large numbers helped strengthen anti-Semitism (Bibó 1986). In 1948, the Communist Party itself added to the problems: under Soviet influence it launched an anti-Semitic campaign that ultimately led to the arrest and detention of well-off Jews and then even of communist Jews, including the leaders of the religious community. The JOINT in Hungary was forced to close down, while the Zionist movement, which had gained strength in Hungary in the aftermath of the war, was banned. The attacks on institutions of Jewish identity were synchronous with a decrease in the number of war-crime investigations.

The main identity-forming element of postwar Hungarian Jewish identity became an awareness of wartime persecution, of the Holocaust. The Holocaust gave rise to several distinct feelings and reactions: an all-encompassing *ressentiment* of one's milieu, a persistent suspicion of the outside world, anxiety (angst), a collective sense of loneliness, self-loathing, and a desire to be freed of the burden of Jewish identity (Karády 1992). Most Jewish Hungarians found themselves in a paradoxical situation: although they had lost any feeling of belonging to the Jewish people, other Hungarians continued to view them as "a separate group," as Jews. Thus for many Jews, Jewish identity took on a kind of reactive nature. That is to say, many felt that it was the reaction of the majority that forced them to regard themselves as Jews (Kovács 1988).

A characteristic feature of political justice in the postwar period was a belief in the capacity of law to change the ethical norms of society. In view of all the evidence of postwar anti-Semitism in Hungary (for the pogroms, see Pető 2009d), we had no reason to expect, however, that the change of regime in 1945 might have altered the public mentality. At the same time, it was evidently the absence of a clear stance by the state that ruled out such a development. In this chapter we showed how such a symbolic and normative position was never taken. This failing by the

Hungarian state then determined the Jewish survivors' view of the Holocaust as a part of their own personal histories. It did so in part because the people's tribunals were unable to fulfill the role assigned to them. An additional factor was that the authorities failed—often intentionally—to provide even symbolic compensation to Jewish victims. The best evidence of this is Act VII of 1946 on "the democratic constitutional order and the criminal legal defense of the republic." The act explicitly permitted the authorities to clamp down on those who "incite national, racial or religious hatred," but this—as the title of the law indicates—was linked with the communist authorities' attempts to deal with opponents of the incipient totalitarian regime. In this chapter we have shown that the country's political leadership rarely used the existing legislation to make clear that anti-Semitism was unacceptable; in general, where this happened, it was merely a "byproduct" of a "defense" of the communist regime.

We often wrongly assume that memory (the formation of memory) was frozen during the Cold War period and did not undergo development and transformation. In this chapter we have argued that the experience of participating in trials held by the people's tribunals as witnesses, judges, lawyers, or spectators contributed to the formation of Jewish survivors' identity. The post-World War II political justice process was the most important bridge between structural and historical trauma (Szaidel 2011, 248). An analysis of the court cases prior to and at the very beginning of the Cold War has revealed a potential for understanding how the awareness and identity of Holocaust survivors developed. The aim was to prove that the crimes committed against Jews were unique. We argue that cases related to crimes against Jews did have a special profile in the legal system. As Szaidel has argued, "structural trauma is based on a history without subjects.... And the price to be paid for such an approach is the dismissal of historical trauma (i.e., the specifics and the particularities of the event itself)" (Szaidel 2011, 251). The individual level, the self, cannot be constructed on a structural level. The universal and particular levels of victims' consciousness are incompatible. It is no surprise that the construction of the Jewish self was happening in such a way during these very difficult times.

Gil Eyal's two forms of the will to memory may assist us in understanding how the justice system affected individuals: "Memory is the guarantor of identity and maintains it through time... memory plays a role in overcoming psychic trauma and the processes of dislocation it sets in motion" (Eyal 2004, 7). We have seen in the case of Hungarian Jews that the memory of the Holocaust became the primary determinant of identity rather than a means of processing trauma, owing above all to the manner in which this memory was treated by the Hungarian justice system and the experiences of Jews as participants in this system. This Jewish identity was reactive and negative. This was evidently the result despite the opportunities available to a large number of active Jews as participants in Hungary's post-World War II juridical process. The manner in which political justice was administered—full of grievances and half-solutions—resulted in the development of the first type of memory.

In the administration of political justice in postwar Hungary, the punishment of the country's former right-wing and extreme right-wing coincided with the expansion of the Stalinist political regime. As time passed—similarly to the situation in other European countries—the political and moral importance of the crimes committed against Jews decreased. As a consequence of this process, in Hungarian collective memory, war criminals and the victims of Stalinism became indistinguishable. However, at the level of the family and the individual, everyone was portrayed as a victim, regardless of whether the defendant brought before the court was a war criminal, a drunken anti-Semite, or the communists' ideological enemy (see Pető 2009d).

The "identity in hiding" thus became entrenched, and the exclusivist approach that one is either perpetrator or victim has, in the course of time, transformed the memory of the Holocaust into a divided memory, whereby, owing to the structural asymmetry, the victim loses twice.

Summary

In this volume we have reviewed the people's justice process in Budapest in the aftermath of World War II. Our systematic quantitative analysis has revealed some surprising facts that were ignored in earlier works.

The first is the characterization of the era. We cannot speak of a single era; rather, it seems that two periods "slipped together" like tectonic plates. First was an immediate postwar period of restoring accountability, and afterwards was a period of abusing the justice system for the purposes of the communist takeover and the replacement of the country's political elite. These two periods have different legal and sociological characteristics. The legal cases related to wartime criminal acts lasted as long as two years, whereas the ideological trials tended to be concluded much more quickly.

The findings of our research will be of interest to future researchers. A particularly important finding was the high proportion of women defendants. We also found that the women often came from established middle-class backgrounds; in other words, the perpetrators were not young and inexperienced. Here we return to the people's tribunals as a device to replace the political elite. We showed that cases of the third type characteristically featured a higher percentage of people belonging to the elite and that these cases often related to collaboration with the Germans. The elite share in the other types of cases was significantly smaller, and so—to use Christopher Browning's expression—it was often the "simple" people who were put on trial (Browning 1992). We found that people from rural areas were overrepresented among defendants found guilty of membership in the Arrow Cross or an associated organization. Lacking other networks, they seem to have been attracted to the Arrow Cross by the opportunities for enriching themselves and for self-realization. Ethnic cleansing is often accompanied by crimes against property, as under such circumstances people can rob and steal with impunity. It is a favorable milieu for those who seek the redistribution of goods (Naimark 2001, 8). An important finding was the high participation rate in this process of established middle-aged people from middle-class and upper-middle-class backgrounds, many of whom had been born outside Hungary's Trianon borders. These were people who had begun new lives in Horthy's Hungary and whose success was derived from their receptiveness to radical right-wing extremism.

The witnesses in the trials were the invisible ones in the justice process. Previous research had ignored them, and yet they clearly influenced the course of justice. Here too the middle-aged were the most numerous: the average age of the witnesses was 41 years. In cases related to membership in the Arrow Cross, we found that a higher proportion of witnesses were rejected by the judges, and this illustrates an underexplored dimension of the transitional justice system: To what extent did it reflect individual circumstances, thereby violating the principle of equality before the law? Defendants of higher social status could often exploit their social contacts and capital to obtain more moderate sentences. Meanwhile, female defendants were more likely than male ones to receive lenient sentences.

A characteristic feature of the political justice system in Hungary was that it was established very early on; when the first trials were held, military conflict was still raging in the western part of the country. This was the pre-Nuremberg period, and the accused were Hungarians. As a result of the history of the Holocaust in Hungary, many Jewish survivors sought justice in the aftermath of liberation. It is this process that researchers have long avoided, perhaps put off by the taboos surrounding the subject. However, our quantitative research has revealed the contradictory experiences of Jews who—as witnesses or aggrieved parties—placed their hopes in the proper and just operation of the people's tribunals. We have also revealed the consequences for Jewish identity of the failures of the transitional justice system.

Another critical element of the post-World War II justice system is the high acquittal rate: 43 percent of all cases ended with acquittals. This means either that innocent people were put on trial (which also means that the real perpetrators went unpunished) or that the trials were inadequately prepared. In the introduction to the volume, we touched upon the extent to which opinion is divided on the effectiveness of the people's tribunals. The data clearly show that around half of all cases ended in acquittal; thus one cannot claim that the tribunals were too strict or severe. Of course, we should also nuance this conclusion by recognizing that there were differences in the rate of acquittal according to the type of trial. Acquittals were far less likely in cases involving well-known politicians, as the political authorities wished to make an example of them. This was not so in the thousands of "minor cases." Many people took part in such cases. An important consequence of the people's justice process was that—as all the various data show (see Pető 2006)—1 in 10 Hungarians came into direct contact with the people's tribunals as defendants or as witnesses. Tens of thousands experienced the arbitrary, inconsistent, and sloppy approach of the people's tribunals at a time when the country was still living under the spell of a fresh start in the aftermath of war. Such experiences—crimes that went unpunished and the relativization of rules and regulations—formed a basic element of these people's political socialization. And although that generation is slowly disappearing from our midst, the long-term consequences of the stories remain with us. We have attempted in this book to map out the post-World War II justice process in Hungary, to understand how memory develops and evolves, and to face up to the consequences.

Bibliography

Albrich, Thomas, Winfried R. Garscha, and Martin Polaschek, eds. 2006. *Holocaust und Kriegsverbrechen vor Gericht. Der Fall Österreich.* Innsbruck, Vienna, and Bozen: Studienverlag.

Alexandrov, G.N., ed. 1969. *War Criminals Must Be Punished: International Conference on the Persecution of Nazi Criminals.* Moscow: Novosti Press Agency.

Bankier, David, and Dan Michman, eds. 2010. *Holocaust and Justice: Representation and Historiography of the Holocaust in Post-War Trials.* Jerusalem: Yad Vashem; New York: Berghahn Books.

Barna, Ildikó, and Andrea Pető. 2007. "A csúnya asszonyok. Kik voltak a női háborús bűnösök Magyarországon?" [The ugly women. Who were the women war criminals in Hungary?] *Élet és Irodalom 51*, no. 43: 10.

Battini, Michele. 2007. "To Prosecute and Portray the Enemy: An Introduction to the American Edition." In *The Missing Italian Nuremberg: Cultural Amnesia and Postwar Politics.* Edited by Stanislao G. Pugliese. New York: Palgrave Macmillan, 1–25.

Bell, Christine, and Catherina O'Rourke. 2007. "Does Feminism Need a Theory of Transitional Justice? An Introductory Essay." *International Journal of Transitional Justice 1*, no. 1: 23–44.

Bernáth, Zoltán. 1993. *Justitia tudathasadása. Népbíróság nép nélkül, a nép ellen* [The schizophrenia of Justitia. A people's tribunal without and against the people]. Budapest: Püski Kiadó Kft.

Bibó, István. 1986. "Zsidókérdés Magyarországon 1944 után" [The Jewish question in Hungary after 1944]. In *Válogatott tanulmányok,* 2nd ed. Edited by Tibor Huszár. Budapest: Magvető, 623–797.

Bloxham, Donald. 2001. *Genocide on Trial: War Crimes Trials and the Formation of Holocaust History and Memory.* Oxford: Oxford University Press.

———. 2004. "From Streicher to Sawoniuk: The Holocaust in the Courtroom." In *The Historiography of the Holocaust.* Edited by Dan Stone. Basingstoke: Palgrave Macmillan, 397–420.

Braham, Randolph L. 1994. *The Politics of Genocide: The Holocaust in Hungary.* New York: Columbia University Press.

Browning, Christopher R. 1992. *Ordinary Men: Reserve Police Battalion 101 and the Final Solution in Poland.* New York: HarperCollins.

Christenson, Ron. 1986. *Political Trials: Gordian Knots in the Law*. New Brunswick, NJ: Transaction Publishers, 10–11.
Conway, Martin. 2000. "Justice in Postwar Belgium: Popular Passions and Political Realities." In *The Politics of Retribution in Europe: World War II and Its Aftermath*. Edited by István Deák, Jan Tomasz Gross, and Tony Judt, 133–156.
Cowen, Tyler. 2006. "How Far Back Should We Go? Why Restitution Should Be Small." In *Retribution and Reparation in the Transition to Democracy*. Edited by Jon Elster. Cambridge: Cambridge University Press, 17–32.
Damaska, Mirjan R. 1986. *The Faces of Justice and State Authority: A Comparative Approach to the Legal Process*. New Haven, CT: Yale University Press, 73–88.
Deák, István. 2006. "Political Justice in Austria and Hungary after World War II." In *Retribution and Reparation in the Transition to Democracy*. Edited by Jon Elster. New York: Cambridge University Press, 124–146.
Dean, Martin. 1999. *Collaboration in the Holocaust: Crimes of the Local Police in Belorussia and Ukraine, 1941–44*. New York: Palgrave Macmillan.
Dimitru, Diana. 2014. "An Analysis of Soviet Postwar Investigation and Trial Documents and Their Relevance for Holocaust Studies." In *The Holocaust in the East: Local Perpetrators and Soviet Responses*. Edited by Michael David-Fox, Peter Holquist, and Alexander M Martin. Pittsburgh: University of Pittsburgh Press, 142–157.
Douglas, Lawrence. 2001. *The Memory Judgement: Making Law and History in the Trials of the Holocaust*. New Haven and London: Yale University Press.
Elster, Jon. 2006. "Retribution." In *Retribution and Reparation in the Transition to Democracy*. Edited by Jon Elster. New York: Cambridge University Press, 32–56.
Erős, Ferenc. 1992. "A zsidó identitás szerkezete Magyarországon a nyolcvanas években" [The structure of Jewish identity in Hungary in the 1980s]. In *Zsidóság, identitás, történelem*. Edited by Mária M. Kovács, Yitzhak M. Kashti, and Ferenc Erős. Budapest: T-Twins Kiadó, 85–96.
Eschebach, Insa. 2003. "Gespaltene Frauenbilder. Geschlecht-dramaturgien im Juristischend Diskurz ostdeutscher Gerichte." In *"Bestien" und "Befehlsempfänger." Frauen und Manner in NS-Prozessen nach 1945*. Edited by Ulrike Weckel and Edgar Wolfrum. Göttingen: Vandenhoeck & Ruprecht, 95–116.
Etmektsoglou, Gabriella. 1998. "Collaborators and Partisans on Trial: Political Justice in Postwar Greece." In *Keine "Abrechnung," NS-Verbrechen, Justiz und Gesellschaft in Europa nach 1945*. Edited by Claudia Kuretsidis-Haider and Winfried R. Garscha. Vienna and Leipzig: Akademische Verlagsanstalt, 231–257.
Exeler, Franziska. 2013. "Reckoning with Occupation: Soviet Power, Local Communities, and the Ghosts of Wartime Behavior in Post-1944 Belorussia." PhD dissertation, Princeton University.
Eyal, Gil. 2004. "Identity and Trauma: Two Forms of the Will to Memory." *History and Memory* 16, no. 1: 5–36.
Feferman, Kiril. 2003. "Soviet Investigation of Nazi Crimes in the USSR Documenting the Holocaust." *Journal of Genocide Research* 5, no. 4: 587–603.
Frei, Norbert, Dirk van Laak, and Michael Stolleis, eds. 2000. *Geschichte vor Gericht. Historiker, Richter und die Suche nach Gerechtigkeit*. Munich: Beck.

Frommer, Benjamin. 2005. *National Cleansing: Retribution against Nazi Collaborators in Postwar Czechoslovakia*. Cambridge: Cambridge University Press.

Gawron, Edyta. 2010. "Amon Goeth's Trial in Cracow: Its Impact on Holocaust Awareness in Poland." In *Holocaust and Justice: Representation and Historiography of the Holocaust in Post-War Trials*. Edited by David Bankier and Dan Michman. Jerusalem: Yad Vashem; New York: Berghahn Books, 281–299.

Gonda, László. 1992. *Zsidóság Magyarországon 1526–1945* [Jewry in Hungary, 1526–1945]. Budapest: Századvég.

Gyenesei, József, ed. 2011. *Pártatlan igazságszolgáltatás vagy megtorlás. Népbíróságtörténeti tanulmányok* [Impartial justice or revenge. Essays on the history of the people's tribunals]. Kecskemét: Adria Print.

Hammer, Brandon. 2007. "Masculinity and Transitional Justice: An Exploratory Essay." *International Journal of Transitional Justice 1*, no. 3: 1–16.

Hilger, Andreas, Ute Schmidt, and Günther Wagenlehner, eds. 2001. *Sowjetische Militärtribunale. Die Verurteilung deutscher Kriegsgefangener 1941–1953. (1.)* Cologne: Bohlau Verlag.

Karády, Viktor. 1992. "A Shoah, a rendszerváltás és a zsidó azonosságtudat válsága Magyarországon" [The Holocaust, the change of political regime, and the crisis in Jewish identity in Hungary]. In *Zsidóság, identitás, történelem*. Edited by Mária M. Kovács, Yitzhak M. Kashti, and Ferenc Erős. Budapest: T-Twins Kiadó, 23–48.

———. 2002. *Túlélők és újrakezdők. Fejezetek a magyar zsidóság szociológiájából 1945 után* [Survivors and those starting over. Aspects of the sociology of Hungarian Jews after 1945]. Budapest: Múlt és Jövő.

Karsai, László. 2000. "The People's Court and Revolutionary Law in Hungary, 1945–1946." In *The Politics of Retribution in Europe: World War II and its Aftermath*. Edited by István Deák, Jan T. Gross, and Tony Judt. Princeton: Princeton University Press, 233–252.

———. 2004. "The Hungarian Holocaust as Reflected in People's Courts Trials in Budapest." In *Yad Vashem Studies*, vol. 32. Edited by David Silberklang. Jerusalem: Yad Vashem Publications, 59–96.

Kovács, András. 1988. "Az asszimilációs dilemma" [The dilemma of assimilation]. *Világosság 28*, no. 8–9: 605–612.

Kuretsidis-Haider, Claudia, and Winfried R. Garscha, eds. 1998. *Keine "Abrechnung." NS-Verbrechen, Justiz und Gesellschaft in Europa nach 1945*. Leipzig: Akademische Verlagsanstalt, Vienna: Dokumentationsarchiv des österreichischen Widerstandes.

Lukács, Tibor. 1979. *A magyar népbírósági jog és a népbíróságok (1945–1950)* [The law on people's tribunals in Hungary and their operation (1945–1950)]. Budapest: Közgazdasági és Jogi Kiadó, Zrínyi Kiadó.

Major, Ákos. 1988. *Népbíráskodás. Forradalmi törvényesség* [People's justice. Revolutionary legality]. Budapest: Minerva.

Markovits, Inga. 2001. "How the Law Affects What We Remember and Forget about the Past: The Case of East Germany." *Law and Society Review 35*, no. 3: 513–563.

Naimark, Norman. 2001. *Fires of Hatred: Ethnic Cleansing in Twentieth Century Europe*. Cambridge: Harvard University Press.

Nozick, Robert. 1974. *Anarchy, State, and Utopia*. New York: Basic Books.

Olosz, Levente. 2014. *A háborús bűnösök felelősségre vonása a kolozsvári népbíróságon* [The trials of war criminals at the people's tribunal in Kolozsvár]. http://itthon.transindex.ro/?cikk=23651. Last accessed November 23, 2014.

Palasik, Mária. 2000. *A jogállamiság megteremtésének kísérlete és kudarca Magyarországon* [The attempt to establish the rule of law in Hungary and its failure]. Budapest: Napvilág.

Papp, Attila. 2011. "Néptörvényszék, népbíróság és népbírósági jog Magyarországon" [The people's tribunals and the law on people's tribunals in Hungary]. *E-tudomány 9*, no. 4: 1–141.

Pastushenko, Tetiana. 2013. "Sowjetische 'Justice': die Qualifizierung der Zusammenarbeit mit den Nazi-Deutschland in der Sowjetunion, 1941–1955." National Academy of Sciences of Ukraine, Kiev (manuscript).

Paul, Gerhard. 2002. *Die Täter der Shoah. Fanatische Natizionalsozialisten oder ganz normale Deutsche?* Göttingen: Wallstein.

Pelle, János. 1995. *Az utolsó vérvádak. Az etnikai gyűlölet és a politikai manipuláció kelet-európai történetéből* [The last blood libels. Ethnic hatred and political manipulation in Eastern European history]. Budapest: Pelikán.

Penter, Tanja. 2005. "Collaboration on Trial: New Source Material on Soviet Postwar Trials against Collaborators." *Slavic Review* 64, no. 4: 782–790.

Pető, Andrea. 1998. *Nőhistóriák. A politizáló magyar nők története (1945–1951)* [Herstories. The history of Hungarian women in politics (1945–1951)]. Budapest: Seneca.

———. 2006. "Népbíróság és vérvád az 1945 utáni Budapesten" [The people's tribunal and blood libel in post-1945 Budapest]. *Múltunk 51*, no. 1: 41–72.

———. 2007. "Problems of Transitional Justice in Hungary: An Analysis of the People's Tribunals in Post-War Hungary and the Treatment of Female Perpetrators." *Zeitgeschichte 34*, November–December: 335–349.

———. 2009a. "Privatised Memory? Story of Erecting the First Holocaust Memorial in Budapest." In *Memories of Mass Repression: Narrating Life Stories in the Aftermath of Atrocity*. Edited by Nanci Adler et al. New Brunswick, NJ, and London: Transaction Publishers, 157–175.

———. 2009b. "Who is Afraid of the 'Ugly Women'? Problems of Writing Biographies of Nazi and Fascist Women in Countries of the Former Soviet Block." *Journal of Women's History 21*, no. 4: 147–151.

———. 2009c. "Death and the Picture: Representation of War Criminals and Construction of Divided Memory about World War II in Hungary." In *Faces of Death: Visualising History*. Edited by Andrea Pető and Klaaertje Schrijvers. Pisa: Plus Pisa University Press, 39–57.

———. 2009d. "About the Narratives of a Blood Libel Case in Post Shoah Hungary." In *Comparative Central European Holocaust Studies*. Edited by Louise Vasvari and Steven Totosy de Zepetnek. West Lafayette, IN: Purdue University Press, 240–253.

———. 2012. "'I Switched Sides': Lawyers Creating the Memory of Shoah in Budapest." In *Confronting the Past: European Experiences*. Edited by Davor Paukovic, Vjeran Pavlakovic, and Viseslav Raos. Zagreb: Political Science Research Centre, 223–235. (Political Science Research Forum, 10.)

Pezzino, Paolo, and Guri Schwarz, 2007. "From Keppler to Priebke: Holocaust Trials and the Seasons of Memory in Italy." In *Holocaust and Justice: Representation and*

Historiography of the Holocaust in Post-War Trials. Edited by David Bankier and Dan Michman. Jerusalem: Yad Vashem; New York: Berghahn Books, 299–328.

Pogany, Istvan. 1997. *Righting Wrongs in Eastern Europe.* Manchester: Manchester University Press.

Prusin, Alexander V. 2010. "Poland's Nuremberg: The Seven Court Cases of the Supreme National Tribunal, 1946–1948." *Holocaust and Genocide Studies* 24, no. 1: 1–25.

Romijn, Peter. 2000. "'Restoration of Confidence': The Purge of Local Government in the Netherlands as a Problem of Postwar Reconstruction." In *The Politics of Retribution in Europe: World War II and Its Aftermath.* Edited by István Deák, Jan T. Gross, and Tony Judt. Princeton: Princeton University Press, 173–194.

Rousso, Henry. 2006. "The Purge in France: An Incomplete Story." In *Retribution and Reparation in the Transition to Democracy.* Edited by Jon Elster. New York: Columbia University and Cambridge University Press, 89–124.

Szaidel, Natan. 2011. "Suffering as a Universal Frame for Understanding Memory Politics." In *Clashes in European Memory: The Case of Communist Repression and the Holocaust.* Edited by Muriel Blaive, Christian Gerbel, and Thomas Lindenberger. Innsbruck, Vienna, and Bozen: Studien Verlag, 239–255.

Szakács, Sándor, and Tibor Zinner. 1997. *"A háború megváltozott természete"—Adatok és adalékok, tények és összefüggések—1944–1948* ["The changed nature of war"—Data, facts and relationships—1944–1948]. Budapest: Génius Gold.

Wouters, Nico. 2010. "The Belgian Trials (1945–1951)." In *Holocaust and Justice: Representation and Historiography of the Holocaust in Post-War Trials.* Edited by David Bankier and Dan Michman. Jerusalem: Yad Vashem; New York: Berghahn Books, 219–245.

Index

acquittal, 16, 16n7, 33, 77–78, 80–83, 92, 104, 112–113
Act II of 1930 (Military Criminal Code), 15, 15n5
Act V of 1878 (Criminal Code – Csemegi Codex), 14n3, 15, 15n5
Act VII of 1945, 16n8,11, 17, 25n34
Act VII of 1946, 16–17, 19, 22–23, 47–48, 52, 79, 79n75, 80, 100, 108
Act VIII of 1945, 58–59
Act XXXIII of 1896 (Code of Criminal Procedure), 15, 15n5
Act XXXIII of 1912, 15
Act XXXIV of 1947, 17, 19, 25n34, 95, 105n95
acts committed against Jews, 47–51, 51n53, 52, 60, 63, 66, 68, 70, 72, 83, 98, 99–101, 103n92
acts committed against non-Jews, 46, 48, 50, 51n53, 54–57, 61–62, 64, 68–69, 73, 76–78, 83
Allied Powers, 14
anti-fascism, 7
anti-fascist discourse, 2–3
anti-Jewish acts, 46
anti-Jewish law, 106
anti-Jews wartime atrocities, 88
anti-Semitic, 100–101, 101n89, 107
anti-Semitic hate speech, 100
anti-Semitism, 46n51, 48, 52, 107–108
appeal, 8, 10, 14n2, 18, 20, 24–25, 33, 38, 41, 77, 79, 92, 104–105
Armistice Agreement, 14–15, 15n4

Arrow Cross membership/membership in the Arrow Cross (*Nyilaskeresztes Párt*) 42, 46, 48–50, 51, 51n53, 54–55, 58–62, 65, 68, 70–73, 75–77, 77n71, 78, 82, 90, 102, 111–112
Arrow Cross Party *(Nyilaskeresztes Párt),* 9, 42, 42n49, 59–60, 71, 77, 101–102
Austria/Austrian, 8–9
average age, 52, 62, 87, 112

ban on exercising one's profession, 21, 24, 40
Bar Association, 85
Bárd, Károly, 30n37
Belgian Commission for War Crimes, 9
Belgium, 9
Bibó, István, 107
Browning, Christopher R., 111
Budapest, 14, 31, 33–34, 53, 53n55, 54, 63–64, 68, 85, 89, 91, 95, 97, 101, 104, 106, 111
Budapest National Committee, 14, 14n1–2
Budapest People's Tribunal/People's Tribunal of Budapest, 17, 17n12, 33–34, 42–43, 53, 53n55, 63, 95, 98, 103
Bulgaria, 2

Chapter V of the Code of Criminal Procedure, 19
chief public prosecutor, 20

Christenson, Ron, 25
Civil Democratic Party (*Polgári Demokrata Párt*), 19
classification of people's tribunals, 46
closed question, 29
Criminal Code, 14n3, 15, 16, 21n23
Code of Criminal Procedure, 15–16, 19, 20n19
Chapter V of the Code of Criminal Procedure, 19
Section 326 of the Code of Criminal Procedure, 16
Cold War, 97, 100, 108
collaborator, 2, 9–11
collective memory, 86, 106, 109
commerce, 57
communist dictatorship, 48–49
communist takeover, 46, 48, 99, 105, 111
company manager, 57
company owner, 57
compensation, 106, 108
concentration camp, 11, 85
confirmative research, 27
confiscation of assets, 21–22, 22n27, 23–24, 24n 32, 79, 93
control figures, 80
conviction, 11, 41, 78, 82–83, 85, 92, 104
Conway, Martin, 9
corroborative witness, 82
Council of the People's Judge, 14
court, 7–12, 14, 14n2–3, 15, 15n4, 17, 20, 22n28, 25, 32–33, 37, 40–41, 46, 53n55, 77, 77n71, 85–86, 92, 96–97, 100–102, 104, 108–109
court hearing/hearing, 7–10, 33, 40, 71–72, 75, 77, 93–94, 105
court-paid lawyer/ appointed public defender, 4, 69, 69n67, 70, 70n67, 71, 74–76
courts of law, 37
Criminal Code (Csemegi Codex), 14n3, 15
Section 92 of the Criminal Code, 15
Section 105 of the Criminal Code, 16

criminal liability (and punishability) of minors, 24
Csősz, László, 30n37
Czechoslovakia, 9

data sheet, 32–33, 36, 38, 40–41
database, 36–39, 39n47, 40–41
database relating to the court hearings, 40
database relating to the defendants, 39
database relating to the witnesses, 40
Deák, István, 8
Decree no. 5900/1945 ME9 and Decree no. 6750/1945 ME, 16
Prime Ministerial Decree no. 1440/1945 ME, 16
Prime Ministerial Decree no. 15 of 1945, 21n22
Prime Ministerial Decree no. 81/1945, 14
defendant, 1, 4, 11, 16n7, 18, 18n14, 19–20, 20n17, 22–24, 28–30, 33, 35–36, 37n45, 38–39, 39n47, 40–43, 46, 50–54, 54n56, 55–60, 65–66, 66n65, 67–68, 68n66, 69–70, 70n77, 71–77, 77n71, 78–81, 81n76, 83, 86–88, 88n81, 89–93, 96, 100n87, 101–102, 105, 109, 111–113
male defendant, 60, 88–90, 92
multiple defendants, 38, 50, 71–72
only one defendant/single defendant, 36, 38, 50, 77n71
women/female defendant, 42, 86–87, 88, 88n81, 89–93, 101–102, 111–112
defense, 16, 19, 20n17, 22n28, 24, 77, 83, 100, 108
defense lawyer, 24, 83
demographic characteristics, 77, 103
denunciation, 9, 49–51
deportation, 10, 97, 106
disability, 57
disciplinary sanctions, 21
discrepancy in data, 43, 59, 65, 89
domestic servants, 57

Index

dynamic data, 35

Eastern Europe, 8, 10
education, 40, 55, 55n58, 56, 64, 70–71, 74, 77, 81, 89–90, 101
    educational qualification, 55n58, 64, 77, 81
    eighth–grade education/elementary, 55, 55n58, 89
    less than eight grades education/elementary 55, 55n58
    level of education/educational level, 40, 55–56, 70, 74, 81, 89–90, 101
    no education/schooling, 55, 74
Elster, Jon, 2
encoder, 28n36, 29–32, 36, 36n42, 38, 41, 45, 56
encoding method, 29, 36
Europe/ European, 7, 9, 23, 97, 109
execution, 14
expert roundtable/roundtable discussion, 30, 30n37, 31
explorative research, 27
Extraordinary State Commission on Reporting, 11
Eyal, Gil, 108

fascism, 106
Fedák, Sári, 87
Feferman, Kiril, 11
female war criminal, 86–87
female/woman lawyer, 71n68, 85–86
female/women, 2, 38–39, 42, 51–52, 57, 61, 65–66, 74, 81, 85–86, 87n78, 88, 88n79, 88n81, 89–96, 101–104, 111–112
female/women people's judge, 93–95
First Amendment to the PMDPJ, 16–18, 20–22, 24, 79n75, 105n95
forced labor, 10, 13, 22, 22n26, 40, 79, 99
France, 2, 9–10
Gáspár, Lili, 86
gender, 4, 36, 38–40, 51–52, 61–62, 65, 66, 71, 81, 85–88, 88n79, 90–91, 96, 101

generalization/generalized, 27, 28, 34, 38, 85
genocide, 11, 46
Germany/German, 8–11, 42n49, 46, 58, 58n63, 59n64, 90, 111
ghettoization, 106
Greece/Greek, 10

hatred (ethnical, racial or religious), 100, 108
head judge, 18, 18n14, 19, 19n16
historical canon, 87
historical memory, 87
historical trauma, 108
history of the people's tribunal, 1, 3, 85
Holocaust, 4, 7, 46, 63, 97–98, 103, 105, 107–109, 112
Horthy regime, 13, 86, 105
Hungarian, 1, 4, 7–8, 15, 15n4, 16n8, 17, 17n13, 19–20, 20n18–19, 22, 25, 31, 37, 46, 55n58, 59n64, 85–86, 95, 97, 101, 105–109, 112–113
Hungarian Communist Party (*Magyar Kommunista Párt*), 4, 17, 17n13, 20n18, 95
Hungarian National Independence Front (*Nemzeti Függetlenségi Front*), 17, 20
Hungarian Workers' Party (*Magyar Dolgozók Pártja*), 95
Hungary, 1, 2, 8–9, 11, 13–15, 15n4, 17, 25, 25n33, 37n44, 42–43, 47, 52n54, 54, 54n57, 55, 58n63, 85, 87, 96–100, 102, 105–107, 109, 112–113
hypotheses, 27, 34

ideological collaboration, 9
ideological trial, 47–51, 57, 62, 67–68, 70–72, 83, 94, 100, 103, 111
imprisoned, 8–10
imprisonment, 9–10, 79
inaccuracy of estimation (statistical error), 42
Independent Smallholders Party (*Független Kisgazdapárt*), 17, 20, 95

indictment, 16n7–8, 19, 22, 33, 35, 37, 41, 45, 45n50, 46n51, 49, 51, 80–81
institutionalist approach, 2
internment, 11, 21–22, 40
interwar (Hungarian) society, 56–57
investigation, 2–4, 11, 15, 22n28, 25, 34, 35, 43, 45–46, 52, 71, 80–81, 93, 99, 102, 107
Italy/Italian, 2, 10

Jewish, 4, 8, 10, 27n35, 46–47, 52, 63, 70, 75, 88, 97–103, 103n91–92, 104–109, 112
Jewish identity, 4, 27n35, 97, 99, 101, 103–105, 107, 109, 112
Jewish survivor, 8, 97–98, 104–106, 108, 112
Jews, 9–11, 28, 33, 45–46, 46n51, 47, 47n52, 48–50, 51n53, 52, 54–57, 60–73, 75–78, 82–83, 94, 97–100, 100n88, 101, 101n89, 102–103, 103n92–93, 104–109, 112
JOINT, 107
judgment, 2, 13–14, 14n2–5, 15, 16n7–8, 17–18, 20–21, 23–24, 35, 37, 40–41, 49, 77–82, 82n77, 83, 92, 104
court judgment, 92, 104
final judgment, 78–79, 82–83
judiciary process, 7
jurisdiction, 15, 16n8, 21–22, 22n25, 22n28, 25, 53
Justice Minister, 105
justice system, 1–2, 4, 13, 25, 28, 85–86, 96–97, 105, 107–109, 111–112

Kádár, Gábor, 30n37
Karsai, László, 27n35, 35n40, 98–100
Kecskemét, 86
Koncz, Erzsébet, 86
Kovács, András, 30n37

labor camp, 99
law on people's tribunals, 14–15, 23, 25
lawmaker, 13, 22
lawsuit, 13, 22

lawyer, 4, 15, 19, 24, 30, 33, 69–70, 70n67, 71, 71n68, 74–76, 83, 85–86, 105, 108
Legal Prosecution of Collaborators, 10
liberation, 2, 8–10, 112
loss of job, 21–22, 40, 79
loss of public office, 23
Lukács, Tibor, 14–15, 16n8, 20
Lüdtke, Alf, 2

Main Commission for Investigation of German Crimes, 11
Major, Ákos, 13n1, 14, 14n3, 15n4, 105
male/men, 13–14, 38–39, 51, 60, 71, 81, 85–87, 87n78, 88, 88n79, 89–93, 96–97, 102, 112
Markovits, Inga, 2
maximum-security prison, 21, 79, 93, 96
measurement, 30
membership in the Arrow Cross (*Nyilaskeresztes Párt*) or an associated organization, 46, 49–51, 51n53, 54–55, 57, 61–62, 65–66, 68, 73, 82, 111
memory, 1–3, 7, 86–87, 97–98, 101, 106, 108–109, 113
Military Criminal Code, 15, 15n5
military guard, 86
military officer, 86
minimum-security prison, 15, 15n6, 21n24, 40, 79, 93, 96
Ministry of Justice, 8, 10
monetary fine, 15, 21–22, 24, 40, 79
Moscow, 14–15
multi-dimensional analyses, 41, 43
murder, 10, 13, 52, 89, 100

National Council of People's Tribunals/ National Council (*Népbíróságok Országos Tanácsa*), 18, 19n15, 20–21, 24
National Peasants Party (*Nemzeti Parasztpárt*), 17n13, 20n18, 95–96
National Trade Union Council (*Országos Szakszervezeti Tanács*), 18, 20, 95, 105n95

Index

Nazi, 8–9, 11
Netherlands, 10
non-commissioned officer, 57
not valuable statement/worthless statement, 74, 76
Nozick, Robert, 106
nulla poena sine lege, 23
nullum crimen sine lege, 23

occupation, 8, 10–11, 30, 37, 37n45, 56–57, 57n60, 64, 86
Örkény, Antal 30n37
overrepresentation, 52–53, 55, 58, 62, 64–68, 70, 72–73, 76, 81, 89–90, 101, 104

paid lawyer, 4, 69, 69n67, 70, 70n67, 71, 74–76
Papp, Attila, 14, 15
pardon, 10, 16, 33
penitentiary, 15n6, 21–22, 22n26, 40, 79–80, 93, 93n83
people's justice, 13–15, 111, 113
people's judge, 14, 17–18, 18n14, 19n16, 86, 93–94, 94n84, 95, 105, 105n95
people's tribunal, 1, 3–4, 12–14, 14n3, 15–16, 16n8, 17, 17n12, 18–19, 19n15, 20–21, 21n22, 22–25, 25n34, 27, 27n35, 28, 31, 33–35, 38, 40, 42–43, 45–47, 50–53, 53n55, 60, 63, 71–72, 77, 79n75, 80–81, 85–86, 92, 94–100, 103, 103n92, 104–106, 108, 111–113
people's tribunal case file, 28, 38
people's tribunal council, 18–20
perpetrator, 11, 50–51, 58, 85–88, 96–98, 109, 111–112
female/women perpetrator, 51, 86–87, 96
male perpetrator, 85
persecuted person, 46
Pest County, 53n55
petition, 18–19, 49–50
PMDPJ (Prime Ministerial Decree on People's Justice), 14–15, 15n5, 16–18, 18n14, 19, 19n16, 20–21, 21n22, 22–25, 37, 59n64, 79n75, 80, 95, 105n95
First Amendment to the PMDPJ, 16–18, 20–22, 24, 79n75, 105
preamble to the PMDPJ, 17
Second Amendment to the PMDPJ, 19, 19n16, 20, 24–25, 80, 95
Section 1 of the PMDPJ, 23
Section 3 of the PMDPJ, 21, 21n22
Section 3 of the First Amendment to the PMDPJ, 21
Section 6 of the PMDPJ, 22
Section 11 of the PMDPJ, 37
Sections 11–18 of the PMDPJ, 22
Section 13(4) of the PMDPJ, 59n64
Section 15 of the First Amendment to the PMDPJ, 24
Section 19 of the First Amendment to the PMDPJ, 18
Section 19 of the PMDPJ, 22
Section 20 of the PMDPJ, 22
Section 21 of the First Amendment to the PMDPJ, 24
Section 21 of the PMDPJ, 21
Section 22 of the PMDPJ, 24
Section 24 of the PMDPJ, 19
Section 36 of the PMDPJ, 19
Section 37 of the PMDPJ, 17
Section 39 of the PMDPJ, 17
Section 42 of the PMDPJ, 18
Section 49 of the PMDPJ, 18, 18n14
Section 50 of the PMDPJ, 18–19, 19n16
Section 53 of the PMDPJ, 24
Section 54 of the PMDPJ, 20
Section 56 of the PMDPJ, 20
Section 57 of the PMDPJ, 20
Poland/Polish, 11
police, 22, 22n25, 57, 104
Polish Supreme National Tribunal (NTN), 11
political administration, 10, 12
political criminal act, 21
political elite, 9, 13, 85, 111
political justice, 1–3, 7, 11, 46, 85–86, 96, 98, 104, 106–109, 112

political prosecutor/lay prosecutor, 19
political trial, 25
post-Shoah, 105
postwar acts, 49–50, 52–53, 56, 59, 61–62, 70–71, 73, 75–80, 83, 88, 88n80, 92, 94, 101, 103
post-World War II, 1, 7, 13, 31, 47, 51, 85, 106, 108–109, 112–113
pre-1945 regime, 95
pre-Nuremberg period, 112
Prime Ministerial Decree (ME), 14, 16, 16n9–10, 17
Prime Ministerial Decree on People's Justice (PMDPJ), 14
pro-German, 46
provision of law, 37, 80
public discourse, 1, 87
public history, 1
public life, 1, 86–87
public prosecutor, 16n9, 19–20, 24, 86
public servant (public official), 16n10, 57
public service, 57
punishment, 2, 4, 15n6, 16n8, 21, 21n22, 22, 22n25, 23, 23n30, 24, 33, 48, 79–80, 93, 93n82, 96, 101, 109
primary punishment, 21
secondary punishment, 21–23

qualitative, 31, 35, 96
quality of the data, 34
quantification, 28
questionnaire, 28–32, 34–36

Rajk, László, 25, 25n33
random number generator, 34
random sampling, 34
reliability, 16n7, 30–32
religious denomination/affiliation, 102, 103n93
research description, 1, 3–5, 7–9, 11–12, 27, 27n35, 28–32, 32n38, 33–35, 35n40, 41, 43, 46, 53, 77, 81, 85, 96, 98–100, 102, 111–112
    pilot research, 29, 32, 34

quantitative research, 9, 28, 31, 34–35, 43, 81, 96, 112
    research phase, 32–33
    research project, 27–28, 31, 33
Ries, István, 105
Romania, 12
Romijn, Peter, 11
Rotyits, Péter, 13, 13n1
Rousso, Henry, 9

sample, 16n8, 28–29, 33–34, 39–40, 42–43, 48, 50–51, 53–54, 54n56, 56–58, 60–65, 70, 72–74, 76–78, 81, 86, 88, 90–91, 93–94, 99n86, 101
sampling method/procedure, 29, 34, 42–43
screening, 2, 11, 34
Second Amendment to the PMDPJ, 19, 19n16, 20, 24–25, 80, 95
sectoral level, 57
sentence, 2, 8–11, 14, 14n2, 15n6, 18, 22, 24, 24n32, 30, 33, 35, 40–41, 49, 78–79, 79n75, 80–81, 92, 93, 93n83, 96, 112
sexual crime, 96
Shoah, 98, 105
show trial, 25, 71, 80
Social Democratic Party (*Szociáldemokrata Párt*), 17n13, 20n18, 95
social hierarchy, 57
social status, 4, 55–57, 57n60, 58, 64–65, 68–69, 71, 73–75, 77, 80–81, 101, 112
sound file, 31, 45
Sovietization, 11
Soviet Union/Soviet, 8–11, 42n49, 46, 99, 105, 107
special councils (at the people's tribunals), 17, 22
SS, 59, 59n64
SS „Hunyadi" Division, 59
Stalinist political regime, 109
statement, 4, 12, 31, 34, 39, 74–76, 83, 102, 104–105
static data, 35

structural trauma, 108
survivor, 7–8, 97–98, 104–106, 108, 112
suspension of political rights, 21, 22, 22n27, 23, 40, 79
system of people's tribunals, 14, 16–17, 27, 98
Szaidel, Natan, 108
Szálasi, Ferenc, 42n49, 87
Szívós, Sándor, 13

test-run, 32
trauma, 108–109
Trianon Peace Treaty, 52
Trianon borders, 42, 54–55, 112
types of cases, 38, 49–50, 59, 69, 72–73, 82–83, 100
types of sentence, 40, 79
types of trial/trial types, 45, 47–48, 51–58, 60–74, 76, 78, 94

unarmed labor battalion, 97
underrepresentation, 52, 63–64, 94, 104
Ungár, Margit, 85

valuable statement/applicable statement, 12, 74, 76
value, 43, 99n86, 100, 103
verbal anti-Semitism, 48, 52
Vichy regime, 9
victims of Stalinism, 109
victims' stories, 3
violence, 51, 85, 90, 98
Volksbund, 58, 58n63, 59, 77n73, 90
vote, 18, 18n14, 19n16

war crimes and crimes against the people, 21–22, 22n28

war criminal, 9, 11, 13, 15, 15n4, 21n20, 42n49, 59n64, 86–87, 109
wartime acts, 45, 47, 49–50, 51n53, 52, 54–55, 57, 59–62, 64–73, 75, 77–80, 82, 88n80, 92, 94, 100–103, 103n92, 104
wartime acts against Jews, 45, 47, 50, 51n53, 52, 54–55, 57, 60–62, 64–65, 67–69, 71–73, 75, 77–78, 82, 94, 100–103, 103n92, 104
Wehrmacht, 59
witness, 1, 30, 33, 35, 38, 40, 43, 45–46, 57n60, 60–66, 66n65, 67–69, 72–75, 75n69, 76–7, 77n71, 82, 82n77, 83, 90–91, 97, 102, 102n90, 103, 103n91–92, 104, 108, 112–113
  incriminating witness, 73, 82, 82n77, 83
  Jewish witness, 63, 103, 103n91–92, 104
  neutral witness, 73
  non-Jewish witness, 103–104
  number of witness, 33, 60, 61, 77, 82, 103n92
  supporting witness, 73–75, 82, 82n77, 83
witness statements/statements of witness, 75–76, 83, 102
Woller, Hans, 10
working-class/working class, 57–58, 65, 68–69, 73–74, 86, 104
World War II, 1–4, 7, 13, 25, 27, 31, 45, 47, 51, 71, 85, 87, 98, 105–106, 108–109, 111–113
Wouters, Nico, 9

Zionist movement, 107

For Product Safety Concerns and Information please contact our EU representative GPSR@taylorandfrancis.com Taylor & Francis Verlag GmbH, Kaufingerstraße 24, 80331 München, Germany

Printed and bound by CPI Group (UK) Ltd, Croydon, CR0 4YY

20/03/2026

02075481-0001